The *Ulysses* Guide

Robert Nicholson was born and lives in Dublin. He studied English Language and Literature at Trinity College, and since 1978 has been the curator of the James Joyce Museum at the Joyce Tower in Sandycove. He is also curator at the Dublin Writers Museum in Parnell Square. *The Ulysses Guide* was first published in 1988, establishing him as an authority on the locations of Joyce's novel, and in 2007 he wrote and presented a DVD for Arts Magic, *James Joyce's Dublin: The Ulysses Tour*. He is a founder member of the James Joyce Cultural Centre as well as a former chairman of the James Joyce Institute of Ireland. He is a regular contributor to *The James Joyce Broadsheet*.

D1250245

The *Ulysses* Guide

Tours Through Joyce's Dublin

Robert Nicholson

NEW ISLAND

THE ULYSSES GUIDE
First published 1988
This edition published 2015
by New Island Books
16 Priory Hall Office Park
Stillorgan
County Dublin
Republic of Ireland

www.newisland.ie

PRINT ISBN: 978-1-84840-452-6
EPUB ISBN: 978-1-84840-453-3
MOBI ISBN: 978-1-84840-454-0

British Library Cataloguing Data. A CIP catalogue record for this book is available from the British Library

Typeset by JVR Creative India
Cover design by www.sinedesign.net
Printed by SPRINT-print Ltd.

Contents

List of Illustrations   1

Acknowledgements   3

Foreword to the 2015 Edition   5

Introduction to the 2002 Edition   7

Ulysses: The Episodes   12

Tour 1   *Telemachus, Nestor*   14

Tour 2   *Nausikaa, Proteus, Hades, Wandering Rocks (vii, iv)*   29

Tour 3   *Calypso, Ithaca, Penelope, Wandering Rocks (iii, i, ii)*   59

Tour 4   *Circe, Eumaeus, (Ithaca), Lotuseaters, Wandering Rocks (xvii), Oxen of the Sun*   80

Tour 5   *Wandering Rocks (xv, ix, xvi, x, xiii, xi, xiv, viii), Sirens*   115

Tour 6   *Aeolus, Laestrygonians, Scylla and Charybdis, Wandering Rocks (vi, v, xviii)*   142

Tour 7   *Wandering Rocks (xix)* – The Viceregal Cavalcade   179

Tour 8   *Wandering Rocks (xii), Cyclops*   193

Notes   213

Appendix I   The Movements of Leopold Bloom and Stephen Dedalus on 16 June 1904   215

Appendix II   *Ulysses*: The Corrected Text   219

Appendix III   Joyce's Schema and the Episode Titles   221

Appendix IV   Stephen's Morning Itinerary   223

Bibliography   225

Index   227

List of Illustrations

1. Sandycove Point
2. Sandycove Point in 1904 (Joyce Tower/Bord Fáilte)
3. The Star of the Sea Church, Sandymount
4. Irishtown Road
5. The Crampton Memorial (Dublin Civic Museum)
6. Glasnevin Cemetery
7. The Mater Hospital, Eccles Street
8. St Francis Xavier's Church
9. Aldborough House
10. The O'Brien Institute
11. Amiens Street Station
12. Tyrone Street (Royal Society of Antiquaries of Ireland)
13. Beresford Place
14. Eden Quay and Butt Bridge
15. Brady's Cottages (Royal Society of Antiquaries of Ireland)
16. St Andrew's Church
17. The National Maternity Hospital, Holles Street (Nat. Maternity Hospital)
18. City Hall
19. Eustace Street
20. Grattan Bridge

21. The Chapterhouse of St Mary's Abbey (Dúchas/The Heritage Service)
22. O'Connell Street (formerly Sackville Street)
23. O'Connell Bridge
24. Westmoreland Street
25. College Green
26. Grafton Street
27. Parkgate
28. The Four Courts
29. Foster Place
30. James's Street (Guinness Brewery Museum)
31. Barney Kiernan's (Dublin Civic Museum)

Photographs, except where otherwise stated, are reproduced by courtesy of the National Library of Ireland from the Lawrence, Eason and Keogh Collections. The maps were drawn by Neil Hyslop.

A Note on the Maps

For the sake of clarity, only the most useful and essential details are included on the maps. The reader may find it helpful to study an Ordnance Survey street map of Dublin for additional information on street names and peripheral detail. The principal route on each map is indicated with a bold line, while a broken line signifies a detour or link route. Alternate arrows pointing in opposite directions indicate that this part of the route is retraced in reverse.

Acknowledgements

No work relating the action of *Ulysses* to its locations can be complete without reference to Clive Hart and Leo Knuth's excellent *Topographical Guide to James Joyce's Ulysses*, which identifies all addresses mentioned in the book and supplies some useful comment on the timing of each chapter. In 2004 this enormously helpful work reappeared in a new and improved form, compiled by Clive Hart and Ian Gunn with Harald Beck, under the title *James Joyce's Dublin: A Topographical Guide to the Dublin of James Joyce* (published by Thames & Hudson). I am indebted to the many new insights and information provided by this book, and also to the past few years of contributions and discussions by its authors and the various other members of the 'Ulysses for Experts' web group. Further useful information has emerged from the Irish national census for 1901 and 1911, placed online by the National Archives and available to all at www.census.nationalarchives.ie, and from *James Joyce Online Notes*, edited by Harald Beck and John Simpson at www.jjon.org. I am also indebted to Danis Rose's article in the *James Joyce Quarterly*, establishing the timing of *Nestor* and *Proteus* and the itinerary of the latter. Other sources are listed in the bibliography.

For permission to reproduce photographs from the invaluable Lawrence Collection in the National Photographic Archive, I am grateful to the Trustees of the National Library of Ireland.

My particular thanks are due to the late Patrick Johnston, Curator of the Dublin Civic Museum, to Peter Walsh, formerly Curator of the Guinness Brewery Museum, and to Con Brogan in the Photographic Unit of Dúchas, the Heritage Service, for photographs and valuable information; to Des Gunning and his successors in the James Joyce Cultural Centre, for helpful research; to Gerard O'Flaherty, Vincent Deane and other members of the James Joyce Institute of Ireland, for points of information; to the Photographic Department, Bord Fáilte, for assistance; and to my colleagues in Dublin Tourism for help of various kinds.

Foreword to the 2015 Edition

Since the previous edition of *The Ulysses Guide* appeared in 2002, Dublin has gone from boom to bust. The Celtic Tiger years strewed the city with spectacular buildings and ambitious developments, many of them in the docklands area (hailed, incidentally, as 'the new Bloomusalem' by Taoiseach Charles Haughey at the opening of the International Financial Services Centre). While some of the Joycean locations have succumbed to the march of progress, others have managed to retain their identity, and there are even examples of resurrection. Olhausen's has disappeared from Talbot Street, but Sweny's pharmacy has survived closure and is preserved as a Joycean landmark. Barney Kiernan's, formerly a fading memory, has regained something of its original appearance, and trams are running again in Dublin.

In addition to the tram, followers of this guide now have further means of exploring Joyce's metropolis. The recently introduced Dublinbikes rental scheme gives travellers the opportunity to pick up a pair of wheels at stations throughout the city centre and follow some of the longer routes without wearing out shoe leather or being swept off course in motor traffic. For those immobilised or abroad, or confirmed desk potatoes, there is now the option of Google Street View, which has been extended to most of the streets in Dublin (but not, so far, to all of the itineraries described in *Ulysses*). Since the expiration of copyright restrictions in 2012, there are also numerous apps, kits, aids, guides and tours which aspire to open Joyce's work to a wider audience.

Reading *Ulysses* and exploring Dublin are two forms of the same process. Even as a confirmed resident of both the book and the city I make daily discoveries about each of them, in the most familiar passages as well as those that remain labyrinthine and challenging. If Dublin is no longer structurally the city that I knew at the beginning, so too *Ulysses* now seems to be different as more of it becomes apparent, and with every new reading it takes on a new complexion. I am grateful to the companions, both on the pavement and on the page, who have supported me in my explorations, and I am grateful to New Island for the excuse and the encouragement to go out and do it all again.

Robert Nicholson

Introduction to the 2002 Edition

The Guide

When James Joyce wrote *Ulysses*, he did so with a copy of Thom's Dublin Directory beside him and a precise idea in his head of the location of every action described in the book. The city of Dublin, more than any scholarly work of reference, is the most valuable document we have to help us appreciate the intricate craftsmanship of *Ulysses*. To follow the steps of Leopold Bloom, Stephen Dedalus and their fellow Dubliners from one landmark to the next has become an act, not merely of study, but of homage. It is, in effect, a sort of pilgrimage.

This guide is intended to enable pilgrims, be they scholars, students or ordinary readers, to follow the action of *Ulysses* as near as possible to the locations in which it is set. To facilitate the traveller, it is arranged on an area-by-area basis rather than taking the episodes in sequence. The eight itineraries, which vary in length from one to two hours, occasionally overlap, and indications are given of how to link one route with others nearby. All are designed to be followed on foot except those of the funeral procession (Tour 2) and the viceregal cavalcade (Tour 7). Some of them begin or end conveniently near to a DART station. At certain points detours or extensions are suggested to places of Joycean or general interest. For those unfortunate enough to be precluded by distance or lack of mobility from a physical act of exploration, this book may still help with the visualisation of the time and space within which Joyce's characters move.

Incorporated in the guide is an outline of the action of *Ulysses* as it is presented in each episode. It concentrates on the activities and movements of the characters throughout the day that is described (as distinct from memories, imaginings and ideas) and is, of course, intended neither as a substitute for, nor as an interpretation of, *Ulysses* itself. Page numbers in the margin refer to the standard Corrected Text of *Ulysses* (see Appendix II), but the guide may be followed using any edition of the novel.

There are many popular misconceptions about *Ulysses*, one of them being that the book describes a walk by Leopold Bloom which can be followed continuously from one chapter to the next like some sort of tourist trail. Bloom's day is no stroll. He covers a total of about eight miles on foot and a further ten by tram, train and horse-drawn vehicle. Of certain periods of the day there is no definite account at all, and much occurs between chapters which is simply not described. The guide fills in these gaps as far as possible, and a table is appended charting the known movements of Bloom and Stephen over the course of the day.

Finally, there is one puzzle in *Ulysses* which this guide makes no attempt to solve, namely how to 'cross Dublin without passing a pub'. Maybe you will be in one when you read this.

The Changing City

Since 1904 (and even since 1988 when this guide first appeared) Dublin has altered considerably. Buildings have gone, streets have been renamed, and shops and businesses continue to change hands. Some – but only a part – of this transformation is due to the destruction caused by the Easter Rising of 1916, the War of Independence which followed, and the Civil War of 1922-3. The ravages of these events were confined to certain streets and public buildings, some of which have been restored to their original appearance. Much more widespread is the effect of the gradual removal of old houses, sometimes piecemeal and sometimes by entire blocks, which has been taking place increasingly – and especially during the booms of the 1960s and the 1990s – to make way for new property development. Many old buildings which have been preserved have also been freshened up and deprived of the shabbiness which was characteristic of Joyce's Dublin.

In Bloom's time the streets were laid with cobbles or setts; main thoroughfares had tram-tracks, standards and overhead cables; motor cars were a rarity (only one appears in *Ulysses*) and most people walked, cycled or took the tram. Without the roar and fumes of present-day motor traffic, it was possible to converse in the street as so many of Joyce's characters do, and to cross the roadway at any point without the benefit of traffic lights. Horse-drawn vehicles, however, were plentiful, and the streets were presumably foul with dung, except at the established crossings, where a line of granite setts would be kept clean by sweepers. Dublin was lit by gas; façades were not obscured by plastic and neon signs; there were no television aerials. Shopfronts were more discreet, less flashy; most shops had awnings to shade them from the sun. Most of the city's fine stone buildings were blackened and grimy with coalsmoke. Without trees, traffic islands or painted lines, Dublin's wide streets appeared even wider. Plastic bags and bottles, parking meters, traffic notices, drink cans, bilingual street signs and burglar alarms were other unknowns.

Letterboxes were red, bearing the royal cipher VR or EviiR; now painted green, some of these older boxes may still be found here and there in Dublin. Coins of the period, particularly the large copper pennies, were still in circulation up to decimalisation in 1971 – twelve pence to the shilling, twenty shillings to the pound. The guinea, worth twenty-one shillings, was a unit frequently used for fees and prices. The pound disappeared from the Irish purse in 2002 at a rate of one euro and twenty-seven cent.

Number 7 Eccles Street has gone. Barney Kiernan's has gone, and so have the *Freeman's Journal* office and Bella Cohen's brothel. Much, however, remains – the banks, the public buildings, all the churches and nearly all the pubs mentioned in *Ulysses* are still there. Even Olhausen's the butcher's and Sweny's chemist shop still survive. Many of the original buildings have altered little, despite changes of ownership. Businesses move or disappear so frequently nowadays that street numbers are included in many of the addresses given in the Guide to aid identification.

It is easy to fall into the nostalgic trap of thinking of 'Joyce's Dublin' as a city in a golden age – a time of sepia photographs, parasols, penny tramfares and the leisurely clop of horses' hooves. What we rarely see in the old photographs are the barefoot children, the rampancy of tuberculosis and rickets, the squalor of tenement life and the infamous brothels of Nighttown. Standards of hygiene and personal cleanliness were lower. The shirt which Bloom wears throughout that hot day under his black waistcoat and funeral suit will probably be worn again the next day with the cuffs turned over and a clean detachable collar. Public toilets were of the most rudimentary kind and were not provided for women. Though the poor and the intoxicated are always with us, they were there even more in Bloom's day. 'Dear, dirty Dublin' was the provincial capital of a neglected country, and if independence, prosperity and cosmopolitanism have changed it, it is not altogether for the worse.

Those who read *Ulysses* will know that Joyce was recording not merely the Dublin of 16 June 1904, but the quality of Dublin that survives through everchanging forms. This guide provides the facts of Bloomsday; by using it the reader may also discover the enduring Dublin of then and of today.

Robert Nicholson

Ulysses: The Episodes

1. *Telemachus* 8 a.m. The Tower, Sandycove (Tour 1)
2. *Nestor* 9.45 a.m. The School, Dalkey Avenue (Tour 1)
3. *Proteus* 10.40 a.m. Sandymount Strand (Tour 2a)
4. *Calypso* 8 a.m. 7 Eccles Street (Tour 3)
5. *Lotuseaters* 9.45 a.m. Sir John Rogerson's Quay to S. Leinster Street (Tour 4)
6. *Hades* 11 a.m. Sandymount to Glasnevin (Tour 2b)
7. *Aeolus* 12.15 p.m. The *Freeman's Journal*, Prince's Street, and the *Evening Telegraph*, Middle Abbey Street (Tour 6)
8. *Laestrygonians* 1.10 p.m. O'Connell Street to Kildare Street (Tour 6)
9. *Scylla and Charybdis* 2 p.m. The National Library of Ireland, Kildare Street (Tour 6)
10. *Wandering Rocks* 2.55 p.m. Dublin City
    i. Father Conmee: Gardiner Street to Marino (Tour 3)
    ii. Corny Kelleher: North Strand Road (Tour 3)
    iii. The onelegged sailor: Eccles Street (Tour 3)
    iv. Katey and Boody Dedalus: 7 St Peter's Terrace (Tour 2b)
    v. Blazes Boylan: Thornton's, Grafton Street (Tour 6a)
    vi. Almidano Artifoni: Front Gate, Trinity College (Tour 6)
    vii. Miss Dunne: 15 D'Olier Street (Tour 2b)

viii.   Ned Lambert: The Chapterhouse, St Mary's Abbey (Tour 5b)

ix.   Lenehan and M'Coy: Crampton Court to Wellington Quay (Tour 5)

x.   Mr Bloom: Merchants' Arch (Tour 5)

xi.   Dilly Dedalus: Bachelor's Walk (Tour 5)

xii.   Mr Kernan: James's Street to Watling Street (Tour 8)

xiii.   Stephen Dedalus: Fleet Street and Bedford Row (Tour 5)

xiv.   Simon Dedalus: Upper Ormond Quay (Tour 5)

xv.   Martin Cunningham: Dublin Castle to Essex Gate (Tour 5)

xvi.   Mulligan and Haines: DBC, Dame Street (Tour 5)

xvii.   Cashel Boyle O'Connor Fitzmaurice Tisdall Farrell: S. Leinster Street and Merrion Square (Tour 4)

xviii.   Master Dignam: Wicklow Street (Tour 6b)

xix.   The viceregal cavalcade: Phoenix Park to Ballsbridge (Tour 7)

11. *Sirens* 3.40 p.m. Wellington Quay to the Ormond Hotel (Tour 5/5a)

12. *Cyclops* 5 p.m. Arbour Hill to Barney Kiernan's, Little Britain Street (Tour 8)

13. *Nausikaa* 8.25 p.m. Sandymount Strand (Tour 2a)

14. *Oxen of the Sun* 10 p.m. Holles Street Hospital to Merrion Hall (Tour 4)

15. *Circe* 11.20 p.m. Talbot Street to Beaver Street (Tour 4)

16. *Eumaeus* 12.40 p.m. Beaver Street to Beresford Place (Tour 4)

17. *Ithaca* 1 a.m. Beresford Place to 7 Eccles Street (Tour 3/4)

18. *Penelope* 2 a.m. 7 Eccles Street (Tour 3)

Tour 1
Telemachus, Nestor

Telemachus, 8 a.m.

The Sandycove Martello Tower, known as the Joyce Tower, stands on a rocky headland one mile south-east of Dun Laoghaire, off the coast road. To get there take the train to Sandycove Station and walk down to the sea, where the Tower on Sandycove Point will be clearly visible. Cars should be parked by the harbour as the Tower is on a narrow road. Turn off Sandycove Avenue at the harbour and walk up past the distinctive white house designed as his own residence by the Irish architect Michael Scott, who also designed the present Abbey Theatre, the central bus station in Store Street and other notable public buildings. Follow the path behind the house leading to the Tower.

> They halted while Haines surveyed the tower and said at last:
> —Rather bleak in wintertime, I should say. Martello you call it?
> —Billy Pitt had them built, Buck Mulligan said, when the French were on the sea. But ours is the *omphalos*.

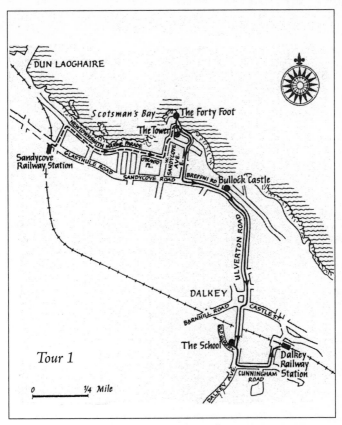

Tour 1

0 ——— ¼ Mile

Coincidentally enough, the order for the building of this tower, and others in the area, was dated 16 June 1804. Altogether about fifty towers of similar design were erected at strategic points on the Irish coast, of which more than half guarded the shores of County Dublin. The name 'Martello' comes from Mortella Point in Corsica, where the original tower was captured, and later copied, by the British. The expected Napoleonic invasion, however, never took place, and

1. Sandycove Point, looking eastwards from the coast road. The ladder may be seen beneath the door of the Tower, and the structure visible to the left of the Tower, behind the rooftop, was an outdoor privy. *Eason Collection EAS 1760, courtesy of the National Library of Ireland.*

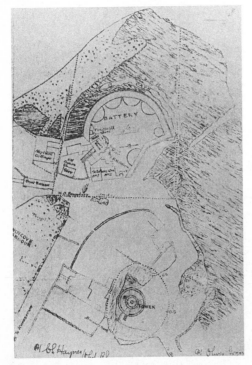

2. Sandycove Point in 1904: A map from the lease signed by Oliver Gogarty. The dotted line around the Tower and battery shows the War Department boundary line with its boundary stones. The 'creek' of the bathing place can be seen to the right of the battery. *Courtesy of the James Joyce Museum.*

most of the towers were demilitarised in 1867. The Sandycove Tower was one of those retained, along with the nearby battery where frequent artillery practice was a source of discomfort, according to Weston St John Joyce (no relative), to nearby residents whose windows were shattered by the concussions.

To their relief the positions were demilitarised in 1897, and in 1904 the Tower was available for rent at the sum of £8 a year. The letting was taken by Joyce's friend and the model for Buck Mulligan, Oliver St John Gogarty, in August 1904. Gogarty's plan was to establish the Tower as an *omphalos* or new Delphi where he could invite other young writers and kindred spirits to join him in the preaching of a modern Hellenism and more convivial pursuits. James Joyce, who arrived on 9 September, was probably more interested in having a roof over his head. His friendship with Gogarty was already cooling and he left precipitately during the night of 14/15 September, never to return.

Gogarty stayed in the Tower regularly, and continued to occupy it up to 1925. Many literary friends visited him there, including George Russell ('A.E.') who painted a picture on the roof, Padraic Colum, Seamus O'Sullivan, Arthur Griffith and possibly also W. B. Yeats, who was reluctantly persuaded to take a swim in the Forty Foot. The Tower might well be known now as 'Gogarty's Tower' had Joyce not used it as the setting for the opening of *Ulysses*. His implication that he himself had paid the rent effectively meant that he stole the Tower for posterity.

The James Joyce Museum, originally run by the Joyce Tower Society, was officially opened by Sylvia Beach, the publisher of *Ulysses*, on Bloomsday 1962. The Society, a voluntary organisation, was brave but unable to carry the financial and administrative burden of running a museum, and within two years it was placed in the hands of the regional tourism organisation. At the time of writing it is still owned and run by Fáilte Ireland, who are proposing to transfer it to Dun Laoghaire–Rathdown County Council; in the interim, by a somewhat Viconian twist, the day-to-day staffing is supplied by volunteers from the recently formed Friends of Joyce Tower Society, who keep it open on a daily basis. For up-to-date information on opening hours, call the museum at (01) 280 9265 or consult a reliable website (www.visitdublin.com or www.joycetower.ie).

Access to the Tower is through the modern exhibition hall, added in 1978. Pass the admission desk and turn right through the new doorway in the base of the tower. At the back of the gunpowder magazine is a narrow spiral staircase leading up to the rooftop, where *Ulysses* begins.

3   'Stately, plump Buck Mulligan came from the stairhead, bearing a bowl of lather on which a mirror and a razor lay crossed. A yellow dressinggown, ungirdled, was sustained gently behind him on the mild morning air.' Around the central gunrest, which Mulligan mounts for his parody of the Mass, and the step beneath the parapet run two rails which supported a gun carriage, swivelling from the pivot in the centre.

Stephen Dedalus, 'displeased and sleepy', follows Mulligan from the stairs and watches as he anticipates the whistle of the departing mailboat (the jet of steam in the harbour would have been visible a couple of seconds before the sound reached the tower). 'Chrysostomos', the word which occurs to Stephen as he observes the gold fillings in Mulligan's teeth gleaming in the sunlight, means 'golden-mouthed', a reference to St John Chrysostomos, who was an early father of the Church and, appositely enough, a namesake of Mulligan and his original, Gogarty, who

4 both have 'St John' as a middle name. While Mulligan shaves, he and Stephen talk about their companion Haines and his nightmare about a black panther. Haines's real-life counterpart was Gogarty's Anglo-Irish friend Samuel Chenevix Trench, and Joyce, as we shall see, had good cause to remember the nightmare. Mulligan then calls Stephen to look at 'The snotgreen sea. The scrotumtightening sea.'

5 'Stephen stood up and went over to the parapet. Leaning on it he looked down on the water and on the mailboat clearing the harbourmouth of Kingstown.' Kingstown, named to celebrate the departure of King George IV in 1821, reverted to its original name of Dun Laoghaire with the coming of Irish independence in 1922. To the east can be seen the Muglins, a small island with a beacon, and on the next point at Bullock is another Martello tower of almost identical design. To the north, on the far side of the bay, is Howth Head, where Bloom proposed to Molly. Nearby on Sandycove Point is the half-moon

battery built with the Tower, beside the Forty Foot bathing place. According to Thom's Directory, most of the houses presently on Sandycove Point were there in Joyce's time. Stephen, however, can only look at 'the ring of bay and skyline' and compare it in his mind to the bowl into which his dying mother

6 had vomited. Mulligan's teasing about his appearance only makes his mood worse as they walk around the Tower arm in arm.

7 'They halted, looking towards the blunt cape of Bray Head that lay on the water like the snout of a sleeping whale.' Bray Head is not, in fact, visible from the Tower – it is to the south beyond Killiney, whose hill with an obelisk is on the skyline – and scholars continue to agonise over whether this is a genuine slip or a deliberate error. Some diehards have drawn comfort from the possibility that the word 'towards' does not necessarily mean that they were looking *at* the Head.

8 Following his argument with Stephen, Mulligan goes downstairs, leaving Stephen to brood alone while the sun, by now somewhere over the Muglins,

9 disappears behind a cloud. His reverie about his mother reaches an anguished climax just as Mulligan returns to bid him to breakfast.

10 Stephen descends halfway down the stairs to enter 'the gloomy doomed livingroom of the tower'. To the left is the fireplace between the two window shafts (called 'barbacans' by Joyce); to the right is the heavy door opened by Haines to let in 'welcome light and bright air' from the sunny side of the

building. It is unused now, and the huge key is on display downstairs. None of the original furniture (mainly supplied by Gogarty from his family home in Parnell Square) remains, but the room has now been refurnished from the evidence of contemporary documents to give an impression of the scene as it was at the time, with a shelf around the walls, a small cooking range and beds in the corners. The floor was in fact wooden rather than 'flagged', and Haines's hammock was probably Joyce's invention as there was nothing to sling it from.

It was here, on the night of 14 September 1904, that Joyce, Gogarty and Trench were sleeping when Trench had a nightmare about a black panther which he dreamed was crouching in the fireplace. Half-waking, he reached for a gun and loosed off a couple of shots to scare the beast away before going back to sleep. Gogarty promptly confiscated the gun. 'Leave the menagerie to me,' he said when Trench's nightmare returned, and fired the remaining bullets at the saucepans over Joyce's head. Joyce leapt out of bed, flung on his clothes and left the Tower immediately. He walked all the way into Dublin and appeared at the National Library at opening time. He never returned to the Tower, and the following evening he and Nora Barnacle made their decision to leave Ireland.

The big door was the only way in and out of the Tower, and was approached by a step ladder attached 11 to the outside wall. As the three men begin their breakfast, Haines sees the old woman coming with the milk, and they have time to exchange a page of dialogue before she reaches the top of the ladder.

> The doorway was darkened by an entering form.
> –The milk, sir!

12 Haines, anxious to try out his Irish on a native, speaks to her in Gaelic, which Joyce does not attempt to reproduce. Haines's original, Trench, was a keen student of the Gaelic Revival and took every opportunity to air his Connemara Gaelic, which was unfortunately marred by a strong Oxford accent.

13 The milkwoman is paid her bill (somewhat reluctantly) by Mulligan and leaves. Mulligan, obviously hopeful of getting money or drink from his friends, urges Stephen to 'Hurry out to your school kip and

14 bring us back some money' and encourages Haines to add Stephen's *Hamlet* theory to his collection of Irish studies. Stephen embarrasses him by asking tactlessly, 'Would I make any money by it?'

15 Mulligan gets dressed and the three leave the Tower to walk to the Forty Foot. Before following their path, it is worth lingering in the Tower to view the collection, which includes several of Joyce's possessions and manuscript items, first editions of *Ulysses* and other works, and all sorts of photographs, paintings and miscellaneous Joyceana. Joyce's guitar, waistcoat and travelling trunk may be seen, as well as one of the two death masks made by the sculptor Paul Speck in Zurich. Among the *Ulysses* trivia are

the key pocketed by Stephen, a Plumtree's Potted Meat pot and an original photograph of Throwaway, the outsider which won the Ascot Gold Cup and indirectly led to Bloom's hasty departure from Barney Kiernan's. The bookshop at the entrance has currently suspended operations but may return to business with the new régime.

16　Leaving the museum, turn left down the path along the top of the cliff, where Mulligan chants his 'ballad of Joking Jesus' on the way to the bathing place.

17　Stephen follows with Haines, foreseeing correctly that Mulligan will obtain the key from him and prevent him returning to the Tower. He explains to Haines how he is the servant of two masters – Britain and the Roman Catholic Church – and a third 'who wants me for odd jobs'; this last, though unspecified, is probably Irish nationalism. In his mind he has a vision of the Church and its banishment of all those who dared contest its dogmas.

18　They followed the winding path down to the creek. Buck Mulligan stood on a stone, in shirtsleeves, his unclipped tie rippling over his shoulder. A young man clinging to a spur of rock near him, moved slowly frogwise his green legs in the deep jelly of the water.

The sign at the entrance to the bathing place once read, ambiguously, 'FORTY FOOT GENTLEMEN ONLY'. The latest wisdom on the mysterious origins of the name suggests that an offshore fishing ground gave the title to what became known as the Forty

Foot Hole. The bathing place itself is only half that depth and has a long and colourful history. Probably established as a men's bathing place by the soldiers of the battery garrison in the early 1800s, it was maintained by regular bathers who in 1880 formed the Sandycove Bathers' Association. The granite screening wall protecting bathers from the east wind and the public gaze was built in the 1890s, while the concrete shelters, erected in 1969, replaced a Victorian structure on the same spot. Still famous all year round for its nude bathers, the Forty Foot has nonetheless been blithely used by both sexes since the 1970s, although the Sandycove Bathers' Association remained by constitution an all-male body up to 2014. In 2015 responsibility for the Forty Foot was taken over by the County Council, and the Association retains only a social rôle.

19   Stephen has awaited the moment when Mulligan will demand the key, and has even gone out of his way to the Forty Foot to give Mulligan the opportunity. Finally he has to prompt him by announcing his departure, and the 'usurper' does what is expected of him.

'—And twopence, he said, for a pint. Throw it there.' Mulligan and Haines arrange to meet him again at The Ship pub, where presumably he will be expected to buy them drink. He leaves them and walks back up the path on his way to Dalkey.

The most direct route, and the one which Stephen probably took, goes by way of Sandycove

Avenue East and left along Breffni Road and Ulverton Road, passing Bullock Castle on the left. The castle, built in the thirteenth century, dates from the time when Bullock Harbour was the principal port of entry to Dublin for traders from abroad. Several castles in this area guarded the port and the lands of rich monasteries round about. The castle is now attached to Our Lady's Manor, a home for elderly people.

At the far end of Ulverton Road is the village of Dalkey, which in Joyce's day was the last stop on the tramline from Dublin. Dalkey has been celebrated by two later Irish writers, Flann O'Brien and Hugh Leonard. Flann O'Brien's comic novel *The Dalkey Archive* (1964) involves a demented scientist named De Selby who plans to destroy the world with a patent substance known as DMP; also featured is James Joyce, who is discovered alive and well and claiming that *Ulysses* was a smutty book compiled under his name by a ghostwriter. Hugh Leonard's plays *Da* (1973) and *A Life* (1980) and his autobiography *Home Before Night* (1979) lovingly recreate the Dalkey of his childhood in the 1930s. A Heritage Centre in the castle in the main street tells the story of Dalkey – including its Joycean connection and other literary links – through exhibits, images and information panels. A visit to the battlements provides a view of the local topography. The Centre is open every day except Tuesday.

Stephen's route continues up Dalkey Avenue as far as the corner with Old Quarry on the right.

Nestor, 9.45 a.m.

20   —You, Cochrane, what city sent for him?
        —Tarentum, sir.

On the corner of Dalkey Avenue and Old Quarry, just a mile from the Tower, is a large, very rambling house named 'Summerfield'. It was once the home of the poet Denis Florence McCarthy (1817–82), whose *Poetical Works* are among the volumes on Bloom's bookshelf (p.582). McCarthy was given to begetting children as well as verses, and the multiple extensions to the house were added as his family grew.

This was the location of the Clifton School, run by Mr Deasy's original, Francis Irwin. Joyce informed his first biographer, Herbert Gorman, that he taught at the school at this address for a short while in 1904, and it is traditionally accepted as the setting of the episode. It is convenient to imagine that the handsome porch was the one referred to by Joyce, that a pocket-sized playfield might have been situated on the tennis court behind the trees to the right of the gate, and that the 'lions couchant' beside the garden steps were transplanted in Joyce's imagination to the tops of the stone pillars at the gate. In fact, although Irwin continued to live in the gate-lodge, the school moved at the end of 1903 to Cintra, a house on the corner of Vico Road at the far side of Dalkey, with none of the features mentioned by Joyce and certainly no space to accommodate a hockey game. There is no independent record of

Joyce serving as teacher at either address. The house and grounds of Summerfield are private.

As the opening episode was imbued with religion, so this one is preoccupied with history. Stephen is teaching history to a class of boys whose names – Cochrane, Armstrong, Talbot and so on – reflect their background. They are all of wealthy middle-class 'West British' families, Protestant probably and more English than Irish. 'Welloff people, proud that their eldest son was in the navy. Vico road, Dalkey.'

21 Neither Stephen nor his pupils are particularly interested in the lesson, and they switch to English
22 and a passage from Milton's *Lycidas*. When the lesson ends he asks them a riddle which they cannot answer and to which the solution is a baffling one:

> Stephen, his throat itching, answered:
> —The fox burying his grandmother under a hollybush.
>
> He stood up and gave a shout of nervous laughter to which their cries echoed dismay.

As countless Joyce scholars have skirted quietly round this one, it seems clear that the boys were not expected to understand it either.

23 The boys leave for hockey and Stephen stays to
24 help Sargent with his sums before joining Mr Deasy in his study to get paid. In the study, which resembles a
25 little museum with its cases of exhibits and curios, the
26 theme of history dominates their conversation. Mr Deasy is proud of his unionist background and the

traditions inherited from the English; Stephen thinks of it as a pageant of bigotry and violence.

27 Mr Deasy finishes a letter for the newspapers which he wishes Stephen to pass on to the *Evening Telegraph*. It proposes a solution to the foot-and-mouth disease
28 and is phrased in a series of time-worn clichés. He then delivers a diatribe against the jews, which prompts a direct comparison of their views of history. To Stephen, it 'is a nightmare from which I am trying to awake'. For Mr Deasy, 'All human history moves towards one great goal, the manifestation of God.'

29 Stephen takes his leave of Mr Deasy, and has got
30 as far as the road when Deasy follows him with a final word:

> —Ireland, they say, has the honour of being the only country which never persecuted the jews. Do you know that? No. And do you know why?
> He frowned sternly on the bright air.
> —Why, sir? Stephen asked, beginning to smile.
> —Because she never let them in, Mr Deasy said solemnly.

Leaving the school, Stephen in all probability walks to Dalkey Station via Dalkey Avenue and Cunningham Road, and takes the train to Lansdowne Road Station. From here he would turn right along Lansdowne Road and Newbridge Avenue (where *Hades* begins) to Sandymount Road, where he walks down Leahy's Terrace to the sea. Tour 2a begins at this point.

Tour 2
Nausikaa, Proteus, Hades,
Wandering Rocks (vii, iv)

Stephen Dedalus probably arrives on the train from
Dalkey at Lansdowne Road Station just opposite the
celebrated rugby ground. James Joyce was living quite
near this station in the spring and summer of 1904,
at rented rooms in 60 Shelbourne Road, just west of
the railway line. His landlady, Mrs McKernan, is mentioned on page 26. On 15 June he was encouraged
to leave until he could find money to pay his arrears
of rent (perhaps the 'five weeks' board' mentioned)
and he moved in for a couple of days with his friends
James and Gretta Cousins (referred to in the same
passage) nearby at 22 Dromard Terrace. A plaque
records that he was staying there on Bloomsday.

Turn right on leaving the station and follow
Lansdowne Road across the River Dodder. Taking
the most direct route towards the beach would have
brought Stephen along the next road to the left,
Newbridge Avenue, and past No. 9 on the left-hand
side, where, a short while later, the mourners were to
gather in the coaches to follow Paddy Dignam on his

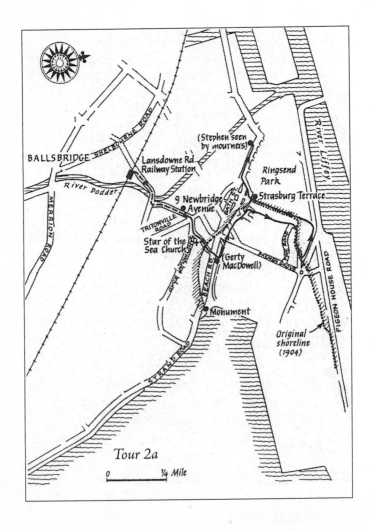

Tour 2a

0 ¼ Mile

last journey. Tour 2b, along the funeral route, starts from this point. To follow Tour 2a, continue across Tritonville Road and along Sandymount Road as far as Leahy's Terrace.

Tour 2a *Nausikaa,* 8.25 p.m.

284   The summer evening had begun to fold the world in its mysterious embrace. Far away in the west the sun was setting and the last glow of all too fleeting day lingered lovingly on sea and strand…

Mr Bloom, who at this stage of the story was last seen leaving Barney Kiernan's at high speed with the citizen's dog in hot pursuit, has spent the past couple of hours visiting Paddy Dignam's widow in Newbridge Avenue. Afterwards he makes his way, presumably by Leahy's Terrace, to the beach. It is now almost sunset, which took place at 8.27 p.m.

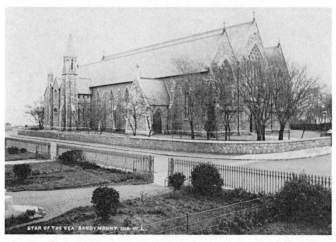

3. The Star of the Sea Church, Sandymount. Five trees, no longer young, now stand alongside the railings of Leahy's Terrace in the foreground. On the extreme left of the picture can just be seen the gap in the wall at the top of the steps leading to the strand. *Lawrence Collection R 1114, courtesy of the National Library of Ireland.*

In 1904 the present Beach Road did not exist. Leahy's Terrace was shorter than it is now, stretching about as far as the wall of Cosy Lodge, and ended in a set of steps leading down to the beach. All of the strand between Beach Road and Pigeonhouse Road has since been reclaimed and built on, making it difficult to locate precisely any of the activities described in this area. Press on, however, across the Beach Road and over the low wall on the other side.

It seems clear that this chapter is set opposite Leahy's Terrace, within sight of the church of St Mary, Star of the Sea, and close enough to hear the singing inside. Gerty MacDowell, Cissy Caffrey and Edy Boardman are seated here on the rocks with baby Boardman in his pram and the twins Jacky and Tommy Caffrey at work on a sandcastle.

285   '…and Master Tommy would have it right go wrong that it was to be architecturally improved by a frontdoor like the Martello tower had.' The Martello tower in question, similar in pattern to the one in Sandycove, would probably be the Sandymount Tower, some distance away just round the corner of the shore on Strand Road.

The first half of the episode is told from the point of view of Gerty MacDowell, in what Joyce described to his friend Frank Budgen as 'a namby-pamby jammy marmalady drawersy (alto là!) style with effects of incense, mariolatry, masturbation, stewed cockles, painter's palette, chitchat, circumlocutions, etc. etc.' It reads in the same way as the cheap romantic magazines which obviously take up a large part of

286 Gerty's reading time. As the heroine, she is described
287 in detail both in appearance and in dress. 'Gerty was
dressed simply but with the instinctive taste of a votary
of Dame Fashion…' These details extend as far as her
288 undergarments, a subject for which Joyce had a special
affection.

289 Gerty's reverie of romance is interrupted by
Tommy Caffrey's bold behaviour and the remarks of
her companions.

290 —I'd like to give him something, she said, so I
would, where I won't say.
—On the beeoteetom, laughed Cissy merrily.
Gerty MacDowell bent down her head
and crimsoned at the idea of Cissy saying an
unladylike thing like that out loud she'd be
ashamed of her life to say, flushing a deep rosy
red, and Edy Boardman said she was sure the
gentleman opposite heard what she said.

291 The gentleman opposite turns out to be Leopold
Bloom, who participates more actively soon
292 afterwards when Jacky Caffrey kicks the ball towards
him; he throws it back and it lands at Gerty's feet. She
293 looks at him and their eyes meet. 'And while she gazed
her heart went pitapat. Yes, it was her he was looking
at, and there was meaning in his look.'

294 The background to their exchange is the
295 Benediction in the Star of the Sea church nearby.
Gerty swings her foot in time to the *Tantum Ergo*,
showing off her stockings, and realises 'that she had
296 raised the devil in him.' Bloom's hand is in his pocket

and he removes it nervously when Cissy Caffrey approaches to ask him the time. It is getting dark. 'Edy began to get ready to go and it was high time for her […] because it was a long way along the strand to where there was the place to push up the pushcar…'

Access to the beach from the higher shore was limited to a number of points where roads or public land met the beach. The steps from Leahy's Terrace were unsuitable for a pushcar, so a gentler slope had to be found, possibly in the direction of Bath Street.

297   Cissy and Edy get the children ready to go. 'And
298 she could see far away the lights of the lighthouse so picturesque…' The lighthouses, now out of view behind trees and buildings, include the Bailey lighthouse on Howth Head, the Poolbeg lighthouse on the South Wall and the lighthouses on Dun Laoghaire harbour to the southeast.

299   As they prepare to leave, the twins see the fireworks shooting up into the sky behind the church, from the bazaar in Ballsbridge to the southwest. Everyone runs down the strand for a better view, except for Gerty, who remains behind, aware that Bloom is gazing at her. 'His hands and face were working and a tremour went over her'. Leaning back to look at the fireworks, she knowingly reveals her legs to him.

300   As a Roman candle flies over the trees Gerty leans further back, displaying 'her other things too, nainsook knickers, the fabric that caresses the skin'. Bloom is given 'a full view high up above her knee' and can contain himself no longer. The fireworks express his sensations. 'And then a rocket sprang and

bang shot blind blank and O! Then the Roman candle burst and it was like a sigh of O! and everyone cried O! O! in raptures and it gushed out of it a stream of rain gold hair threads and they shed and ah! they were all greeny dewy stars falling with golden, O so lovely, O, soft, sweet, soft!'

301   Cissy calls Gerty and she rises to go.

> She walked with a certain quiet dignity char-
> acteristic of her but with care and very slowly
> because – because Gerty MacDowell was…
> Tight boots? No. She's lame. O!

Joyce, no doubt with tongue in cheek, labelled the technique of this chapter 'Tumescence and detumescence'. Everything mounts up to a climax in a grand explosion; deflation swiftly follows, beginning with the revelation of Gerty's defect and the switch from her thoughts to Bloom's point of view. He is left alone, thinking about the ways of women and recomposing his wet shirt. 'My fireworks. Up like a rocket, down like a stick'. Thoughts of women put him in mind of babies and he reminds himself to visit Mrs Purefoy in the maternity hospital. Some of Gerty's perfume lingers in the air. 'What is it? Heliotrope? No. Hyacinth? Hm. Roses, I think. She'd like scent of that kind. Sweet and cheap: soon sour.' He muses about perfume and personal odours and smells himself. 'Almonds or. No. Lemons it is. Ah no, that's the soap.'

His eye is caught by the flashing of the Bailey lighthouse, and he recalls proposing to Molly on

309   Howth Head. 'Where we. The rhododendrons.'
Watching the bat flying about, he thinks sleepily
310   about animals, migrating birds and sailors. 'A last
lonely candle' explodes over the bazaar as nine
o'clock approaches. On the shore, the postman does
his round, the lamplighter lights the gaslight outside
the church, and a newsboy circulates with the *Evening
Telegraph*, attracting the attention of someone in the
Dignam house, probably Master Patrick Dignam,
who was looking forward on page 206 to seeing the
account of the funeral in the paper.

Joyce was particular enough about his details to
write a letter to his Aunt Josephine Murray (Aunt
Sara's original) asking 'whether there are trees (and
of what kind) behind the Star of the Sea church in
Sandymount visible from the shore'.

Another light twinkles at him, from the Kish
lightship far out on the horizon. It has since been
replaced by a permanent lighthouse, which was built
in Dun Laoghaire harbour and towed out to be sunk
in position on the sandbank.

311   Tired, Mr Bloom considers his plans. 'Go home.
Too late for *Leah. Lily of Killarney*. No. Might be still
up. Call to the hospital to see. Hope she's over. Long
day I've had.'

312   Finding a bit of stick, he idly starts to write a
message in the sand for Gerty in case she comes
that way again: 'I… AM. A….', then stops and rubs
313   it out. The noise of the cuckoo clock striking nine
in the priest's house as the chapter ends suggests
that 'CUCKOLD' is the word he left unwritten.

Meanwhile Bloom has allowed himself to nod off for a few minutes. Later he will leave the beach and take the tram as far as Holles Street for his intended visit to Mrs Purefoy.

Proteus, 10.40 a.m.

31   Ineluctable modality of the visible: at least that if no more, thought through my eyes. Signatures of all things I am here to read, seaspawn and seawrack, the nearing tide, that rusty boot.

We return to the morning and Stephen Dedalus, who passes on his way across the strand from Leahy's Terrace the very spot where Bloom was later to come to rest. His thoughts are dominated by the theme of change, as it relates to space (the modality of the visible) and time (the modality of the audible).

The strand itself has been subject to a great deal of change since 1904. Then, it was bounded to the north by the Pigeonhouse Road and to the west by the main drainage embankment along the edge of Ringsend Park, which was at that time in the process of construction. Now, the nearest sand is a good hundred yards away to the southeast, where a standing stone on the shore, designed by Cliodna Cussen and erected in 1983, is dedicated to James Joyce. A smaller stone aligned with it points in the direction of sunrise on the winter solstice. The nearby strand was investigated by Danis Rose, who used the evidence of its seawrack, seaspawn, shells and shingle to plot the course of Stephen's walk.[1]

Stephen is walking away from Leahy's Terrace. By the time he opens his eyes he is below the tidemark, about as far as the path now running parallel to Beach Road. The tide, approaching steadily across the flat strand, is still two hours from its full at 12.42. Looking about him, he observes the two women, the *Frauenzimmer*, who have followed him down from the terrace. 'Number one swung lourdily her midwife's bag, the other's gamp poked in the
32 beach.' Prompted by the sight of the midwife, Stephen imagines himself connected back through all humanity to Eve by a succession of navelcords. 'The cords of all link back, strandentwining cable of all flesh.'

Meanwhile he is walking approximately north-westwards, following the line of the shore. Keep walking along the footpath towards Irishtown. 'His pace slackened. Here. Am I going to Aunt Sara's or not?' Stephen is heading in the direction of his aunt's house in Strasburg Terrace in Irishtown, perhaps with the idea of arranging a place to stay for the night. In his mind's eye he pictures the scene if he should visit.

> I pull the wheezy bell of their shuttered cottage: and wait. They take me for a dun, peer out from a coign of vantage.
> —It's Stephen, sir.
> —Let him in. Let Stephen in.

His uncle Richie is the same Richie Goulding with whom Bloom dines at the Ormond Hotel later in

33 the day. 'Houses of decay, mine, his and all. You told
the Clongowes gentry you had an uncle a judge and
an uncle a general in the army. Come out of them,
Stephen. Beauty is not there.'

34 Musing about the failure of his family and of his
own aspirations, Stephen walks onward. Cross Bremen
Grove to a triangular patch containing the Irish
Mercantile Marine Memorial, and cross again towards
the nearest of the brightly painted Corporation houses.
Nicknamed 'Toytown', this development won a major
European environmental award when it was built in
1982. Follow Kerlogue Road towards Ringsend Park.

The grainy sand had gone from under his
feet. His boots trod again a damp crackling
mast, razorshells, squeaking pebbles…

The backdoors which he sees are probably those in
the area ahead and to his left in Strand Street. Ahead,
across Ringsend Park, he can see the 'wigwams' of
Ringsend on the Liffey docks. 'Ringsend', wrote
Weston St John Joyce in 1912, 'though now presenting
a decayed and unattractive appearance, was formerly
a place of considerable importance, having been
nearly two hundred years in conjunction with the
Pigeonhouse harbour, the principal packet station in
Ireland for communication with Great Britain. The
transfer of the packet service, however to Howth and
Kingstown in the early part of last century, deprived
Ringsend of its principal source of revenue, and
consigned it henceforth to poverty and obscurity.'

'He halted. I have passed the way to aunt Sara's. Am I not going there? Seems not. No-one about. He turned northeast and crossed the firmer sand towards the Pigeonhouse.' Although Strasburg Terrace is now only a short distance ahead of Stephen, he appears to have overshot the access point – a set of steps or a ramp – leading from the beach up to the shore. The route northeast leads across the present sports ground, parallel to the boundary of Ringsend Park, in the direction of the Pigeonhouse Road. The name 'the Pigeonhouse' refers variously either to the fort or to a house standing in the grounds of the electricity power station. Originally on the site was a large strongly constructed wooden house built by the port authorities in the early eighteenth century to hold stores and serve as a watch house. The caretaker, a man named Pidgeon, made his fortune by developing the premises as a popular and exclusive hostelry whose name outlived both Pidgeon and the house.

35   The name reminds Stephen of a passage from Léo Taxil's blasphemous *La Vie de Jésus*, and in turn of his Paris friend Patrice Egan who told him about it. He recalls his year in Paris and his return, summoned by

a blue French telegram, curiosity to show:
—Nother dying come home father.

The 'misprint' was restored only in the Corrected Text.

'His feet marched in sudden proud rhythm over the sand furrows, along by the boulders of the south wall. He stared at them proudly, piled stone mammoth skulls. Gold light on sea, on sand, on boulders.' Cross Pine Road and follow the footpath which runs along the boundary below the pumping station. This is the route that Stephen takes alongside the boulders of the south wall, while he thinks of Paris and Patrice's father Kevin Egan, the exiled Fenian. This leads him directly towards the sea and he soon stops when his feet begin to sink in the wet sand. 'Turning, he scanned the shore south, his feet sinking again slowly in new sockets. The cold domed room of the tower waits.' The Sandycove Tower is out of sight beyond Dun Laoghaire, but Stephen's thoughts may have been prompted by the sight of the similar tower on the other side of the strand. Now, of course, the entire view is obscured by the nearby houses.

36
37

> The flood is following me. I can watch it flow past from here. Get back then by the Poolbeg road to the strand there. He climbed over the sedge and eely oarweeds and sat on a stool of rock, resting his ashplant in a grike.

How far along the edge of the beach Stephen has walked is uncertain, but it is unlikely in the limited time span of this episode that he has got much further than the point where Pine Road now meets Bremen Grove, south of the old coastguard station which stands nearby. Beyond here the original coastline is lost under new roads and a fenced-off field. Behind Stephen as he sits is the long mole running out to the Pigeonhouse. In front of him he sees a dead dog and a sunken boat; approaching from the distance he sees a live dog and, further off, two figures whom he takes at first for the two midwives until he realises that the dog belongs to

38 them. Gradually they come near enough for him to distinguish 'A woman and a man. I see her skirties. Pinned up, I bet.' He sees from their activities that they are cocklepickers. This area, as Weston St John Joyce noted, 'was at one time noted for its cockles and shrimps'. The shrimps disappeared after the hard winter of 1741. 'The cockles, however, still remain for those who have the courage to eat them, and occasionally yield a rich harvest to the profes-sional cocklepickers.'

39 The dog passes nearby and digs in the sand, its claws reminding Stephen of a panther and Haines's nightmare; he then recalls his own dream: 'Open hallway. Street of harlots. Remember. Haroun al Raschid. I am almosting it. That man led me, spoke. I was not afraid. The melon he had he held against my face...'

The cocklepickers pass, 'the ruffian and his strolling mort', and Stephen thinks of a verse written

40 in the 'rogues' rum lingo' of these gypsy folk. A moment later a poem of his own (borrowed, it must be admitted, from Douglas Hyde) begins to form in his mind.

He comes, pale vampire, through storm his eyes, his bat sails bloodying the sea, mouth to her mouth's kiss.

Hunting in his pockets for paper, he finds Deasy's letter and tears off the blank end on which to write the
41 poem. When it is finished, he lies back contemplating the toes of his borrowed boots, and notices the rising tide flowing in from Cock Lake, a pool out in the Strand.

In long lassoes from the Cock lake the water flowed full, covering greengoldenly lagoons of sand, rising, flowing. My ashplant will float away. I shall wait. No, they will pass on, passing, chafing against the low rocks, swirling, passing. Better get this job over quick. Listen; a fourworded wavespeech: seesoo, hrss, rsseiss, ooos.

The 'wavespeech' reproduces the sound of a wave breaking, spreading and receding back across the flat strand; though some scholars have conjectured that Stephen has stood up and is taking the opportunity to urinate. Looking at the water, his thoughts turn to the drowned man, 'Bag of corpsegas sopping in foul
42 brine,' and the 'seachange' he is undergoing. Finally he takes his ashplant, preparing to go. He has left his handkerchief in the Tower, and picks his nose rather than blowing it. Looking behind him over the road, he sees the 'high spars of a threemaster', moving up the Liffey into the port of Dublin, 'a silent ship'.

Stephen plans to return by going up onto 'the Poolbeg Road', i.e. the Pigeonhouse Road which also leads out along the two-mile pier to the lighthouse which Joyce elsewhere calls 'the Poolbeg flasher'. Now painted bright red, it was black in 1904. From the road, he can follow the directions advised by Weston St John Joyce. 'Returning along the Wall, we take the turn on the left along the Rathmines and Pembroke Main Drain embankment [i.e. along the edge of Ringsend Park], which has reclaimed from the sea a considerable tract now being laid out as a public park.' (Nowadays it is not so easy to follow this route. Instead, turn back along the path you are on directly towards the boundary of the Park.)

This route is the most direct one to lead him to Irishtown via Strand Street and the Irishtown Road. It also happens to bring him straight past Aunt Sara's front door in Strasburg Terrace. He reaches Irishtown in time to be spotted by Mr Bloom between Watery Lane (now Dermot O'Hurley Avenue) and the library on the corner. From here he walks into town in the trail of the funeral procession, stopping in College Green to send a telegram to Mulligan before going on to the newspaper office. (For some alternative ideas on Stephen's route and timing, see Appendix IV.)

To follow the entire route of the funeral cortège, start by returning from Strasburg Terrace to 9 Newbridge Avenue and then provide yourself with a carriage or other vehicle.

Tour 2b *Hades,* 11 a.m.

72   Martin Cunningham, first, poked his silkhatted head into the creaking carriage and, entering deftly, seated himself.

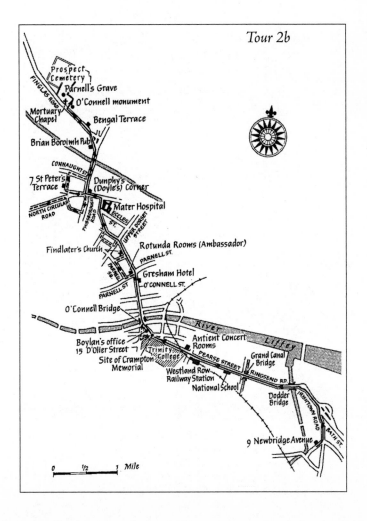

With the introduction of one-way traffic systems it is no longer possible to follow the entire route of the funeral procession by car or horse-drawn cab. Ideally, it may be done by bicycle, dismounting to follow one-way streets on foot where they occur.

The hearse and carriages leave from outside 9 Newbridge Avenue and turn left onto the cobbles of the tramline along Tritonville Road. Harald Beck and John Simpson, in a special study of this chapter[2] have worked out that in all likelihood Bloom is sitting on the right-hand side, facing forward. Opposite him is

4. Irishtown Road. Rattling along this 'cobbled causeway', the funeral carriages pass Dodder Terrace here on the left. At the junction with Bath Street a little further on, the road veers left into Irishtown. Behind the houses in the background, Ringsend Park is under construction. *Lawrence Collection R 10963, courtesy of the National Library of Ireland.*

Martin Cunningham, facing rearwards. Simon Dedalus is sitting beside Bloom, and Jack Power is in the seat diagonally opposite. Their calculations, a total reshuffle of an earlier arrangement proposed by Carole Brown and Leo Knuth, are based partly on the fact that the episode was originally written with Dignam's house located at No. 10, on the opposite side of the road.

—What way is he taking us? Mr Power asked through both windows.
—Irishtown, Martin Cunningham said. Ringsend. Brunswick street.

73   Proceeding along Irishtown Road into Ringsend, the carriage passes Watery Lane (now Dermot O'Hurley Avenue) on the left and then swerves from the tramtrack to travel to the left of the island where a public library now stands. This was probably to avoid the major road works consequent upon the laying down of the new main drainage scheme. At this point, 'Mr Bloom at gaze saw a lithe young man, clad in mourning, a wide hat.' He recognises Stephen Dedalus and points him out to his father.

74   The carriage turns the corner onto Ringsend Road and crosses the humpbacked bridge over the Dodder. A little further on it stops.

—What's wrong?
—We're stopped.
—Where are we?
    Mr Bloom put his head out of the window.
—The grand canal, he said.

The bridge over the Grand Canal was designed to be raised to allow access to the inner canal dock, and this was presumably the reason for the brief halt. On the left beside the bridge is Boland's Mill, popularly confused with the rebel stronghold of Easter 1916 at Boland's Bakery in Grand Canal Street (commanded by Joyce's contemporary Eamon de Valera, who later became Ireland's foremost political leader). The gasworks were across the canal to the right, and the Cats' and Dogs' Home is ahead and to the left. Nowadays the Grand Canal Dock area is surrounded by signature buildings – the Alto Vetro building on the north side of the bridge, and the vast Grand Canal Theatre beside the water to the right.

75   Resuming their journey, the mourners travel over the canal and along Great Brunswick Street (now
76   Pearse Street). They pass on the left St Andrew's National School and Meade's timberyard on the corner of South Cumberland Street, then the 'hazard' or cab rank beside the railway station. 'An hour ago I was passing there,' thinks Bloom. Beside him, next to the tramway standard in the centre of the road, a pointsman switches the points on the tramline near the intersection with Lombard Street.

On the right is the Academy building, formerly the Antient Concert Rooms, which features in Joyce's story 'A Mother' in *Dubliners*. Joyce himself sang there in a concert on 27 August 1904, sharing the bill with such notables as J. C. Doyle and the great Irish tenor John McCormack – both of whom are to take part in Blazes Boylan's concert tour with

Molly Bloom. The original façade has been restored and retained.

Next to the Academy is 'the bleak pulpit of saint Mark's' where Oscar Wilde was baptised in 1854. Further up the street on the left was the Queen's Theatre, now replaced by a modern office block. The Abbey theatre company took up a fifteen-year residence there in 1951 after the old Abbey was destroyed by fire. On the right at No. 27, on the wall above the restored shop-front of the premises of Pearse and Sons, may be seen bas-relief portraits of the monumental sculptor's sons, the 1916 leader Patrick Pearse and his brother Willie, who lived here. The soaring florentine tower beyond it belongs to the Fire Station.

As they near Boylan's office, Bloom thinks helplessly about Molly's assignation. 'He's coming in the afternoon. Her songs. Plasto's. Sir Philip Crampton's memorial fountain bust. Who was he?' The Crampton Memorial, one of Dublin's more extraordinary monuments, stood in the junction at the end of Pearse Street until its semi-collapse in 1959. Because of the botanical nature of the structure, it was popularly known as 'the Cauliflower'. It commemorated Sir Philip Crampton (1777–1858), the Irish Surgeon General. Near its place now stands a stone pillar by Cliodna Cussen, commemorating the fact that this was the original site of the 'Long Stone' erected by the Vikings.

Detour for drivers: All cars except taxis must turn right at Tara Street. To rejoin the funeral route, turn

5. The Crampton memorial. This late photograph shows the back of the sculpture. On the other side, Sir Philip's bust faced up Pearse Street, towards the approaching funeral cortège. *Courtesy of the Dublin Civic Museum.*

left at the river, follow Burgh Quay and turn right onto O'Connell Bridge.

The procession turns right along D'Olier Street (traffic nowadays must continue to Westmoreland Street), passing Blazes Boylan outside the Red Bank Restaurant on the right. The restaurant is now a hostel, Ashfield House, but careful observers may still see the carvings of lobsters and other delicacies on the wall outside.

(188) *Wandering Rocks vii* is set in Boylan's office, believed to be the Advertising Co. Ltd. at 15 D'Olier Street, on the left next to the corner with Fleet Street.

(189) His secretary, Miss Dunne, takes a phone call from Boylan, who is ringing from Thornton's fruit shop. She takes his instructions and passes on a message:

'Mr Lenehan, yes. He said he'll be in the Ormond at four.'

77   'Smith O'Brien. Someone has laid a bunch of flowers there. Woman. Must be his deathday.' The statue of William Smith O'Brien, which once stood at the junction of D'Olier Street, Westmoreland Street and O'Connell Bridge, has been moved further down O'Connell Street to stand between 'the hugecloaked Liberator's form' of Daniel O'Connell and the statue of Sir John Gray.

Passing over O'Connell Bridge, celebrated for being as wide as it is long, they proceed down O'Connell Street (formerly Sackville Street), Dublin's premier boulevard. Although the street has changed in many aspects since 1904, the two most striking changes at street level are the motor traffic (now limited to taxis and buses) and the introduction of a central island running the length of the street and planted with trees. Previously the impression was of a wide open space rather than the channels of today. Outside Elvery's Elephant House, now Kentucky Fried Chicken, on the corner of Middle Abbey Street,

78   they spot Reuben J. Dodd and a story is told about the rescue of Dodd's son from the Liffey when he tried to drown himself. The BBC broadcast this section of the novel in the 1950s and thought it was a great joke when someone claiming to be Reuben J. Dodd Junior brought a libel suit against them. Dodd won his case.

79   'Dead side of the street this.' Bloom is looking at the west side of O'Connell Street north of the GPO as they approach the foundation stone of the

present Parnell Monument (the statue by Augustus Saint Gaudens was unveiled in 1911, twenty years after Parnell's death). The dead are so dominant in this episode that it is appropriate to note the Gresham Hotel on the opposite side, where Gabriel and Gretta Conroy spent the night in 'The Dead'.

Another *Dubliners* location is the Rotunda Concert Rooms (later the Ambassador Cinema, currently an exhibition and entertainment venue) where Mr Duffy met Mrs Sinico in 'A Painful Case'. 'Two Gallants' starts here on 'the hill of Rutland Square', now Parnell Square. Oliver Gogarty's family home at No. 5, opposite the Gate Theatre, is marked by a plaque.

Detour for drivers: Motorists should turn left at the Parnell Monument and turn right around Parnell Square West and North, turning left at Findlater's Church to rejoin the route on North Frederick Street.

The men in the carriage discuss the morality of suicide; only Martin Cunningham knows that Bloom's father poisoned himself. On their left at the top of the hill is Findlater's Church; next door to it at 18 Parnell Square is the Dublin Writers Museum, where Joyce's piano is part of a fascinating collection tracing Ireland's illustrious literary history. The cortège continues up North Frederick Street, over Dorset Street and along Blessington Street into Berkeley Street. Drivers have to turn left into Dorset Street and should turn immediately right along Wellington Street, right at the top along Mountjoy Street past the end of Blessington Street and into Berkeley Street (which becomes Berkeley Road). The mourners pass the top of Eccles Street beside the Mater Hospital. 'The *Mater Misericordiae*. Eccles street. My house down there.'

81 As they turn the corner left onto the North Circular Road they are delayed by a herd of cattle being driven to the docks. They drive onwards to the Phibsborough Road. 'Dunphy's corner. Mourning coaches drawn up, drowning their grief. A pause by the wayside. Tiptop position for a pub.' Dunphy's Corner is now known as Doyle's Corner, and the pub bears the name of John Doyle. The carriages turn right here onto the Phibsborough Road.

Detour for motorists. *Wandering Rocks iv*. Continue to the next turn right onto St Peter's Road. The Joyce family lived on the left-hand side at No. 5 (formerly 7 St Peter's Terrace) in 1904, now marked by a plaque, and it is apparently here that the Dedalus family is in residence.

(186)   Katey and Boody Dedalus shoved in the door of the closesteaming kitchen.
    —Did you put in the books? Boody asked.

Katey and Boody have come from the pawnbroker's in Gardiner Street via Eccles Street, and are given soup by their sister Maggy.

Turn right again round Dalymount Park and rejoin the funeral route on Phibsborough Road.

82   In silence they drove along Phibsborough road. An empty hearse trotted by, coming from the cemetery: looks relieved.
    Crossguns bridge: the royal canal.

The carriages cross the canal and pass the Brian Boroimhe pub. More commonly spelt Brian Boru, this ancient Irish king is another of the commemorated dead who punctuate the funeral route. He is famous for beating the Danes at the Battle of Clontarf in 1014, during which he himself was killed by a Dane who entered his tent while he was praying. Steering left for Finglas Road, they pass the Childs murder house at 36 Bengal Terrace (Mr Power wrongly points to the last house, No. 38) on the right next to the graveyard. The murder of seventy-six-year-old Thomas Childs took place in September 1899; Childs's brother Samuel was charged but acquitted.

83
84 Finally, they draw to a halt at the gate of the graveyard and the mourners walk inside. 'First the stiff: then the friends of the stiff.' The cemetery is open daily from 8.30 a.m. to 5 p.m. for public visits, and a new visitor centre has been opened at the entrance. Dominating the entrance to the cemetery is the O'Connell Monument, a round tower with a 'lofty cone'. To the left is the mortuary chapel, opposite to the tombs of priests and bishops and 'the cardinal's mausoleum'. The cardinal in question was Archbishop McCabe, referred to by Mr Dedalus in *A Portrait* as 'the tub of guts up in Armagh'. 'Billy with the lip' – Archbishop William Walsh – lies nearby. In 1904 the entrance was by the next gate further along the railings and the mourners would have found the chapel and mausoleum to their right.

85 Bloom meets Tom Kernan and Ned Lambert, who were in the other carriage, and the mourners enter the

86   chapel for the funeral service. When it is over they follow the coffincart outside and to the left 'along a lane of sepulchres' and walk towards Dignam's grave. Whereabouts he is buried Joyce does not specify, but the probable area may be reached by walking down the cypress avenue by the chapel, turning left at the

87   bottom, and right at the next intersection. Bloom and Kernan follow Ned Lambert and John Henry Menton,

88   Dignam's employer, and they meet John O'Connell,

89   the caretaker, on the way. By the graveside Bloom looks towards the Botanic Gardens just behind the cemetery and muses about the effect of the corpses

90   on the soil. Nearby he sees the mystery mourner whose identity has intrigued Joyceans ever since. 'Now who is that lankylooking galoot over there in the macintosh? Now who is he I'd like to know?'

91   In the silence after the coffin is lowered he thinks about his own grave nearby: 'Mine over there towards Finglas, the plot I bought. Mamma, poor mamma, and little Rudy.'

92   Joe Hynes of the *Evening Telegraph* approaches Bloom, collecting a list of names.

> —And tell us, Hynes said, do you know that fellow in the, fellow was over there in the…
>   He looked around.
> —Macintosh. Yes, I saw him, Mr Bloom said. Where is he now?
> —M'Intosh, Hynes said scribbling. I don't know who he is. Is that his name?
>   He moved away, looking about him.

The erratic results of Hynes's scribblings may be found on p.529.

Returning by the same route, turn right at the intersection and walk a short distance along the path. On the left is a mound surrounded by an iron railing and surmounted by a huge boulder of Wicklow granite inscribed simply PARNELL. A stone plaque reads 'The Chief's Grave'. Parnell was buried here in 1891. Mourners leaving his funeral plucked ivy leaves from the cemetery wall, and the anniversary of his death on 6 October was celebrated every year thereafter as Ivy Day. Hynes and Mr Power go round this way. Just before Parnell's grave, on the opposite side of the path, is the grave of Joyce's parents. The tombstone, which stands three away from the path, was inscribed according to Joyce's own instructions after his father's death in 1931.

93 Mr Bloom meanwhile walks along 'by saddened angels, crosses, broken pillars, family vaults, stone hopes praying with upcast eyes, old Ireland's hearts and hands', musing over the tombstones and remembering that he will be visiting his father's grave in Ennis on 27 June, the anniversary of his death.

The centenary of Rudolph Bloom's suicide in 1986 was observed by the James Joyce Institute of Ireland, who travelled to Ennis to visit the grave. Unfortunately, as the gardener had long since stopped receiving his annual ten shillings, Rudolph's resting-place could not be found in the undergrowth.

94 'The gates glimmered in front: still open. Back to the world again. Enough of this place. Brings you a

6. Glasnevin Cemetery. The picture shows the O'Connell Monument and the chapel. *Lawrence Collection I 750, courtesy of the National Library of Ireland.*

bit nearer every time. Last time I was here was Mrs Sinico's funeral.' Mrs Sinico's funeral, as we learn elsewhere, took place on 17 October 1903. The story of her death under a train at Sydney Parade Station is related in 'A Painful Case' in *Dubliners*.

95   On the way to the gates Bloom joins Martin Cunningham and John Henry Menton. He points out a dinge in Menton's hat but is treated coldly by Menton, who dislikes him. 'Chapfallen', he follows them to the gates.

It is worth staying awhile to explore the cemetery. Many of Joyce's family, friends and associates lie here, including those who appear as characters in *Ulysses*

– Skin-the-Goat, Michael ('the citizen') Cusack, Father Conmee, J. P. Nannetti and others. In an unusual ceremony in 1988, an elaborate tombstone was placed on the grave of Matthew Kane, the original of Martin Cunningham, whose funeral in July 1904 after his death by drowning was attended by Joyce and his father and is therefore claimed as the original of Dignam's. Some of the most celebrated Irish men and women buried here over the past 150 years are to be found by the east side of the O'Connell Monument. Full information and tours – including one particularly devoted to Joyce and the characters of *Hades* – are available at the museum at the entrance run by the Glasnevin Trust.

From Glasnevin the mourners return by coach to the city centre, where *Aeolus* (Tour 6) takes place. Alternatively, retrace the funeral route to Doyle's Corner, continue through the crossroads and turn right at the lights along Monck Road and Avondale Road. At the top of Avondale Road turn left to follow the North Circular Road as far as Phoenix Park to begin Tour 7.

Tour 3
Calypso, Ithaca, Penelope,
Wandering Rocks (iii, i, ii)

Calypso, 8 a.m.

45   Mr Leopold Bloom ate with relish the inner organs of beasts and fowls. He liked thick giblet soup, nutty gizzards, a stuffed roast heart, liverslices fried with crustcrumbs, fried hencods' roes. Most of all he liked grilled mutton kidneys which gave to his palate a fine tang of faintly scented urine.

Leopold Bloom's house at 7 Eccles Street, one of the most famous addresses in world literature, is now no more. It was situated on the right-hand side as you approach from Dorset Street, approximately opposite No. 76. The site is now marked by a bronze plaque beside the front door of the Mater Private Hospital, with a relevant quotation from *Ithaca*. Once the residence of Joyce's friend J. F. Byrne (the 'Cranly' of *A Portrait*), it was officially listed as vacant in the 1904 Thom's Directory. In later years it became derelict and was half-demolished in 1967. In 1982 it was finally levelled to make way for the

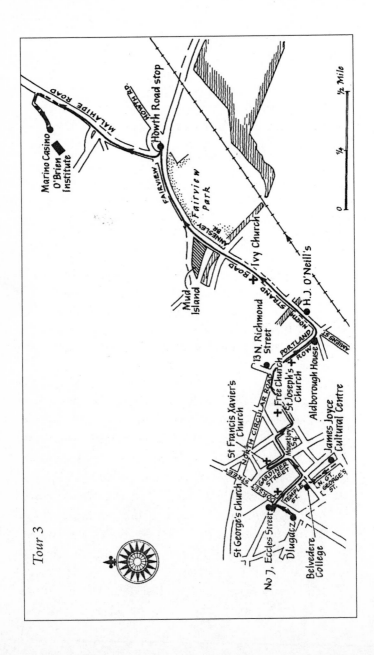

Tour 3

7. The Mater Hospital, Eccles Street. Bloom's house is near the bottom of the street in the terrace on the left-hand side, which has now been replaced by the private wing of the hospital. *Lawrence Collection R 725, courtesy of the National Library of Ireland.*

present building. Bricks and other relics are scattered throughout the Joycean world.

The houses opposite give some idea of its appearance. The kitchen, where Mr Bloom appears at breakfast, was in the basement. He prepares his wife's breakfast tray, gives the cat some milk, goes upstairs to the hall beside the bedroom on the ground floor, and comes out through the front door. 'He pulled the halldoor to after him very quietly, more, till the footleaf dropped gently over the threshold, a limp lid. Looked shut.'

The footleaf, a hinged flap serving as a draught excluder, may be seen on other doors nearby or indeed on the original door of 7 Eccles Street itself, which is on display not very far away in the James Joyce Centre in North Great George's Street.

> He crossed to the bright side, avoiding the loose cellarflap of number seventyfive. The sun was nearing the steeple of George's church.

The cellarflap was a heavy iron disc in the pavement covering the coalhole, through which coal deliveries could thus be made directly from the street. Some of the older Dublin cellarflaps are particularly ornate and of various styles. St George's Church in Hardwicke Place was designed by Francis Johnston in 1802, and Arthur Wellesley, the future Duke of Wellington, was married here in 1806 just before his involvement in the Peninsular War. The bells which chimed on every quarter hour of day or night have been removed to Taney Church in Dundrum, and the building, since relinquished by the Church of Ireland, is now the Temple Theatre.

47
48   Bloom approaches Larry O'Rourke's on the corner, where he turns right into Dorset Street. Restored to its state of Edwardian elegance after years of scruffiness, the pub is now the Aurora gastropub and café. He passes the national school at No. 81-84, now a clinic for the Mater Hospital, and the birthplace of Seán O'Casey at No. 85, and enters Dlugacz's, the pork butcher's, between the school and Blessington Street. This establishment, of which no record exists, was apparently invented by Joyce, who mischievously named it after a Jewish acquaintance in Trieste.

49   Bloom buys a pork kidney and returns towards
Eccles Street, reading a pamphlet, picked from the
butcher's pile of wrapping paper, which advertises
a scheme by a planter's company named Agendath
50 Netaim to buy land near Galilee. A cloud – the same
one, apparently, which Stephen sees from the Tower
on page 8 – covers the sun and sheds gloom on his
thoughts. Further gloom awaits him at his front
door. 'Two letters and a card lay on the hallfloor.
He stooped and gathered them. Mrs Marion Bloom.
His quickened heart slowed at once. Bold hand. Mrs
Marion.' He realises that the letter to his wife is from
Blazes Boylan to make an assignation – a suspicion
which is borne out when Molly does not open the
letter in his presence.

51   His own letter, which he glances at in the kitchen,
is from his daughter Milly in Mullingar. He puts the
kidney on to cook and brings Molly's breakfast upstairs.
52 Here he pauses to explain the word 'metempsychosis'
which she has found, strangely enough, in a trashy
novel named *Ruby: the Pride of the Ring* (identified as
a novel by Amye Reade in which, however, the word
53 does not appear[3]). Smelling the burning kidney,
54 he hurries downstairs to eat breakfast and reread
55 Milly's letter. After breakfast he goes out through the
backdoor, armed with an old number of *Titbits*, and
56 heads for the outdoor lavatory in the garden rather
than 'fag up the stairs to the landing'. 'Asquat on the
cuckstool' he reads the prize story by Philip Beaufoy
57 before using it to wipe himself. As he emerges, the
church bells chime at quarter to nine.

Soon afterwards he leaves to walk to the quays, probably by the same route which he and Stephen follow in reverse in *Ithaca*.

Ithaca, 1 a.m.

544   What parallel courses did Bloom and Stephen follow returning?

545 The itinerary described at the beginning of the episode, leading from Beresford Place via Gardiner Street, Mountjoy Square, Gardiner Place, Temple Street and Hardwicke Place to Eccles Street, may be taken as a variation from Tour 4.

      The chapter, written in the form of a catechism, is at times ludicrously pedantic in style. It also supplies us with the vast bulk of the factual information that can be obtained about Bloom and, to a lesser extent, Stephen. Readers should be aware that despite its magisterial tone it is peppered with errors of fact, science and calculation so numerous that they can be presumed to be deliberate.

546   Arriving at his front door, Bloom realises that he has forgotten to transfer his latchkey to the pocket of his funeral suit (a fact of which he was aware when he went to the butcher's in the morning). 'Bloom's decision?' – 'A stratagem.' He climbs over the railings, down into the area, and enters through the basement 547 door. Stephen is brought in through the front door 548-9 and down into the kitchen. Bloom puts on the kettle, 550 finally uses the lemon soap to wash his hands, and

offers Stephen a wash which he declines ('his last
bath having taken place in the month of October

551-2 of the preceding year'). On the dresser he discovers
traces of Boylan's visit: the fruit basket, a half empty
bottle of port, and 'Four polygonal fragments of two
lacerated scarlet betting tickets, numbered 8 87, 88
6.' He realises at this point the coincidences during
the day which prophesied Throwaway's victory in the
Gold Cup race.

553-4 Bloom makes cocoa and they drink it. We learn of
555 Bloom's early literary compositions, the relationship
between his age (thirty-eight) and Stephen's
556-8 (twenty-two), and other comparisons and links
559 between them. Bloom talks of his ideas for effective
560 advertising; Stephen suggests an advertisement
featuring a piece of paper with 'Queen's Hotel'
written on it. Unknown to him, Bloom's father
poisoned himself in the Queen's Hotel in Ennis,
561 of which he was the proprietor. Stephen tells
562 Bloom 'The Parable of the Plums' which he related
earlier in the day outside the newspaper office; they
563 discuss famous Jews and compare the Jewish and
564 Irish alphabets and languages (of which neither of
them has any practical knowledge). Stephen chants
565 'in a modulated voice a strange legend,' the tale of
566 little Harry Hughes, who has his head cut off by
567 'a jew's daughter, all dressed in green.' Disturbed,
568-9 Bloom thinks about his own daughter Milly.

570 Bloom invites Stephen to stay overnight, but his
571 invitation is declined. He returns Stephen his money,
and they discuss the possibility of meeting for further

572 conversations and mutual instruction. They go out
573 through the backdoor into the garden and observe
the clear summer night sky, 'The heaventree of stars
hung with humid nightblue fruit.'

574 Bloom's scientific mind discards this artistic
575 spectacle and views it prosaically enough as '...an
infinity renderable equally finite by the suppositious
apposition of one or more bodies equally of the same
576 and of different magnitudes.' His contemplation of
the universe is interrupted by the sight of a light in
the bedroom window.

577 At Stephen's suggestion, at Bloom's instigation
both, first Stephen, then Bloom, in penumbra
urinated, their sides contiguous, their organs
of micturition reciprocally rendered invisible
by manual circumposition.

578 Bloom lets Stephen out by the door into Eccles
Lane. Where he goes for the rest of the night is never
579 even stated. Alone, Bloom returns indoors, ascends
the stairs and enters the living room at the front, to
580 find that the furniture has been rearranged. He uses
the Agendath Netaim prospectus to light a cone of
581 incense, and notices that some of the books on the
582-3 shelf are upside down. He rearranges them, sits down
and loosens his clothes.

584 The budget for 16 June 1904 is interesting. It
reveals that Bloom travelled by tram from town to
Sandymount after his bath, and from Sandymount
to town between *Nausikaa* and *Oxen of the Sun*.
More intriguingly, the account omits his trainfare to

Nighttown, the ten shillings he paid on page 455 and the further shilling for the damaged lamp on page 478.

585-91   As a relaxation before retiring, he lets himself think about his ultimate ambition to settle comfortably in a well-appointed residence, and about schemes to

592-3   enable him to afford it. He opens a drawer to place in it his letter from Martha Clifford, whose name and address are also in the drawer, written in a cryptogram which clearly translates as MARTHA/CLIFFORD/ DOLPHINS/BARN. J. F. Byrne, a later occupant of Bloom's house, was an expert on cyphers. This drawer contains a multitude of miscellaneous objects,

594   from cameo brooches to erotic postcards. The other drawer is reserved for certificates and important

595   documents, some relating to Bloom's father, whom

596   they bring to his mind. The financial documents are a

597   security against a situation of poverty, which can only be precluded by death or departure. The possibilities

598   of his departure are considered, including a Missing Person advertisement with his description ('height 5 ft 9 ½ inches, full build, olive complexion').

599-600   He reviews the day briefly and, 'gathering multicoloured multiform multitudinous garments',

601   goes into the bedroom where he puts on his nightshirt and enters the bed. He and Molly have their heads at opposite ends of the bed.

What did his limbs, when gradually extended, encounter?

New clean bedlinen, additional odours, the presence of a human form, female, hers, the imprint of a human form, male, not his, some crumbs, some flakes of potted meat, recooked, which he removed.

Bloom finally finds himself able to consider Boylan's intrusion with equanimity. He is, after all, merely one of a series of men who have found Molly 602-3 attractive. Bloom feels no sense of having 'been outraged by the adulterous violator'. It is, in a strange way, a victory for him.

604 He wakes Molly by a display of affection – 'He kissed the plump mellow yellow smellow melons of her rump, on each plump melonous hemisphere, 605 in their mellow yellow furrow' – and treats her to a carefully modified account of the day's activities. It is only now that we learn that Bloom and his wife 606 have not had complete sexual intercourse since before Rudy's birth more than ten years ago, and that in recent months Molly has taken to questioning Bloom every time he goes out.

607 Finally, Bloom's thoughts melt into confusion and he drifts off to sleep, dreaming about another traveller, Sinbad the Sailor. 'Where?' the last question asks. The answer is a full stop.

Penelope, 1.45 a.m.

608-44 'Yes because he never did a thing like that before as ask to get his breakfast in bed with a couple of eggs...'

Molly Bloom's soliloquy, which has been seen or heard in performance more often than any other episode of

Ulysses, begins where *Ithaca* leaves off. It is divided into eight so-called sentences and is totally unpunctuated apart from one full stop at the end of the fourth sentence and one at the end of the final sentence, ending the book. The full stop on page 624 was in fact only 'rediscovered' in the Corrected Text, and the appropriate thesis about its significance has still to appear. Its position suggests that it acts as a central hinge of some sort.

Because, as Frank Budgen remarks, 'her thoughts jostle one another like the citizens of an egalitarian republic', it is difficult to summarise the episode coherently. Her thoughts swirl about, returning frequently to Boylan and the events of the afternoon, but more and more consistently towards Bloom, whom she finds at turns irritating and endearing.

Much of Molly's day can be pieced together from her thoughts. During the morning, besides rearranging the furniture, she burned a lot of old newspapers and magazines, put the remainder up in the WC, and cleared some old overcoats out of the hall (page 621). In preparation for Boylan's visit she spent 'hours dressing and perfuming and combing' (page 611). At quarter past three, when Katey and Boody Dedalus passed by and the onelegged sailor was begging in the street, she was still in a state of undress whistling 'There is a charming girl I love' in the living room (page 615). Soon afterwards the messengerboy from Thornton's arrived with the port and peaches, and 'I was just beginning to yawn with nerves thinking he was trying to make a fool of me when I knew his tattarrattat at the door' (page 615).

Whether Boylan and Molly paused to rehearse the concert programme before getting down to the main business of the afternoon is not clear. The activity in the bedroom is graphically recalled on pages 611, 617, 620, 621, 633, 638 and 641, the general impression being one of action rather than affection. At some stage they took a break to drink port and eat potted meat. '…he had all he could do to keep himself from falling asleep after the last time after we took the port and potted meat it had a fine salty taste yes…'(page 611).

Boylan also went out to buy an *Evening Telegraph* for the result of the race and came back 'swearing blazes because he lost 20 quid'. He tore up the betting tickets on the dresser where Bloom found them later.

Boylan left, slapping Molly's behind familiarly. After his departure she had a pork chop from Dlugacz's for tea and returned to bed, where she slept soundly until woken by the thunder at ten o'clock.

Boylan occupies relatively little of Molly's thoughts, which revolve mainly round her husband, day-to-day trivia and memories of her girlhood in Gibraltar, her boyfriend Harry Mulvey who kissed her under the Moorish wall, and another early lover, lieutenant Gardner. Her mind shifts from one man to another and the word 'he' can refer to two different men in one line. Her reverie is interrupted by her period – 'O jesus wait yes that thing has come on me yes now wouldnt that afflict you' – and pages 633–4 are delivered from the chamberpot. On page 637 she starts thinking about Stephen Dedalus and the possibility of his becoming a regular visitor. 'I suppose hes 20 or more Im not too old for him if hes 23 or 24'.

The unrefined Boylan is a write-off as far as romance is concerned – 'of course hes right enough in his way to pass the time as a joke' – and in the end it is Bloom that she thinks of and the day in 1888 when he proposed to her on Howth Head. '…and I thought well as well him as another and then I asked him with my eyes to ask again yes and then he asked me would I yes to say yes my mountain flower and first I put my arms around him yes and drew him down to me so he could feel my breasts all perfume yes and his heart was going like mad and yes I said yes I will Yes.'

Wandering Rocks iii, 3.15 p.m.

185   A onelegged sailor crutched himself round MacConnell's corner, skirting Rabaiotti's icecream car, and jerked himself up Eccles street.

The sailor has come from Gardiner Street via Dorset Street. MacConnell's the chemist's at 112 Dorset Street was not actually on the corner itself. He passes the Dedalus girls and stops outside 7 Eccles Street. Molly Bloom, inside in her underwear, flings a coin from the window on the ground floor; the sign *Unfurnished Apartments* refers to the rooms on the floor above.

The line referring to J. J. O'Molloy is an interpolation of a simultaneous event taking place in Meetinghouse

Lane, setting of *Wandering Rocks viii* (page 189). In a similar interpolation on page 205, the sailor reappears in Nelson Street, off Eccles Street.

From Eccles Street, cross Dorset Street and proceed through Hardwicke Place past St George's Church to the bottom of Temple Street North, where there is the opportunity to make a detour to two particularly interesting Joycean landmarks nearby. Turn right at the corner to Belvedere College, the Jesuit school attended by James Joyce from 1893 to 1898 and described in *A Portrait of the Artist as a Young Man*. The college stands at the head of North Great George's Street, a distinctive Georgian thoroughfare where lived Sir Samuel Ferguson, the poet, Sir John Pentland Mahaffy, a famous Provost of Trinity College who associated with Oscar Wilde and Oliver Gogarty, and John Dillon, the Irish Nationalist MP. No. 35, two-thirds of the way down on the left, was formerly the dancing academy of 'Mr Denis J Maginni, professor of dancing &c' (who appears in an interpolation near here on page 181, and later on page 208). The house, finely restored, now leads a new and exciting existence as the James Joyce Centre, which was opened to the public in 1996 as a centre for Joycean study, research and cultural activities. Visitors may take a tour, watch the audiovisual presentation, browse at will in a fascinating library of works by, about and related to Joyce, and visit the exhibition rooms or the Paul Léon Room, where the chairs and table at which Joyce worked in his friend's Paris flat in the 1930s are preserved. They may call in to the bookshop or admire the tearoom murals depicting the eighteen episodes of *Ulysses*. The centre provides regular guided walking tours through areas of Joyce's Dublin and occasional lecture series.

Back at Temple Street, follow Gardiner Place (where a plaque on the Dergvale Hotel commemorates Michael Cusack, founder of the Gaelic Athletic Association and model for Joyce's character 'the citizen') as far as Mountjoy Square. Opposite and to the left is St Francis Xavier's Church (scene of the retreat in 'Grace', the *Dubliners* story). Beyond the church is the presbytery from which Father Conmee emerges at five to three.

Wandering Rocks i, 2.55 p.m.

180   The superior, the very reverend John Conmee S. J. reset his smooth watch in his interior pocket as he came down the presbytery steps. Five to three. Just nice time to walk to Artane.

Father Conmee (1847–1910) was appointed Rector of Clongowes Wood College in 1885, and appears in that position in *A Portrait of the Artist as a Young Man*. He left Clongowes in 1891, the same year that Joyce did (because his father could no longer afford to pay the fees), and was later instrumental in having the Joyce boys educated for free at Belvedere (rather than suffer the awful fate of being educated with 'Paddy Stink and Micky Mud' in the Christian Brothers). In 1898 he was

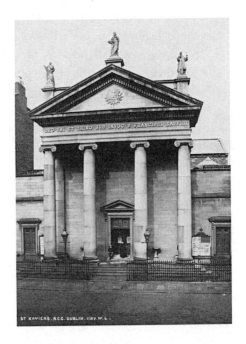

8. St Francis Xavier's Church. Father Conmee passes the church just after five to three. *Lawrence Collection R 1189, courtesy of the National Library of Ireland.*

appointed superior of the St Francis Xavier's community in Gardiner Street, in which rôle he appears here.

He meets the sailor outside the convent on the corner and crosses to Mountjoy Square, where he meets the wife of Mr David Sheehy MP under the trees on the north side. The Sheehys were well known to Joyce, who was a frequent visitor to their home at 2 Belvidere Place. He was particularly friendly with Mary Sheehy, who later married the poet Thomas Kettle. Another sister, Hannah, married Joyce's friend Francis Skeffington, who appears as 'McCann' in *A Portrait*. Skeffington, an ardent pacifist, was arrested and summarily executed during the Easter Rising;

Kettle died in the war in France. A younger brother, Eugene Sheehy, one of the boys in Belvedere, became a prominent judge. His memoir, *May it Please the Court*, contains some entertaining recollections of Joyce.

181   At the corner of Mountjoy Square he meets some schoolboys and gets one of them to post a letter in 'the red pillarbox at the corner of Fitzgibbon street'. Now gone, the pillarbox stood on the north side of the street at the corner. The Joyce family moved to Fitzgibbon Street from Blackrock in 1892; their house at No. 14 on the right is now No. 34. From Mountjoy Square east Father Conmee turns left onto Great Charles Street, where he passes the free church (now the Pavee Point Travellers' Centre) on the left. At the end of the street he turns right down the North Circular Road and Portland Row, passing North Richmond Street on the far side with its Christian Brothers school (13 North Richmond Street, another former Joyce residence, was the setting for 'Araby' in *Dubliners*). On the right he passes St Joseph's Church; the convent 'for aged and virtuous females' attached to the church is now a branch of the Dublin Institute of Technology.

182   'Near Aldborough house Father Conmee thought of that spendthrift nobleman. And now it was an office or something.' Aldborough House, one of Ireland's last Palladian mansions, was built in 1793–6 in the style of William Chambers. Owned in Joyce's time by the Post Office, it is currently empty and disused.

At the Five Lamps, a well known landmark among Dublin illuminations, he turns left onto the North Strand Road, passing Gallagher's at No. 4. Grogan's at

No. 16, Bergin's and Youkstetter's vanished suddenly one night in May 1941 when a German bomber crew mistook Ireland for Britain (the human victims are commemorated in a memorial garden nearby). The buildings have since been replaced by Corporation housing, as was H. J. O'Neill's funeral establishment across the road at No. 164.

(184)   *Wandering Rocks ii* takes place at the undertaker's
(185)   soon afterwards at 3.15. Constable 57C, who saluted Father Conmee, now approaches Corny Kelleher,

9. Aldborough House. Lord Aldborough, 'that spendthrift nobleman', was imprisoned in Newgate Gaol for contempt of the House of Lords. The last of Dublin's great townhouses, this building became the Post Office Stores Department. *Lawrence Collection R 10309, courtesy of the National Library of Ireland.*

an ex-policeman and informer (he comes in handy later in Nighttown when he persuades the policemen to leave Stephen alone). Some information is then exchanged.

Father Conmee crosses the Royal Canal at Newcomen Bridge beside Charleville Mall, and steps into an outward bound tram 'for he disliked to traverse on foot the dingy way past Mud Island.' Mud Island on the left hand side of Annesley Bridge Road, according to Weston St John Joyce, 'was a locality of evil repute in former times…inhabited by a gang of smugglers, highwaymen, and desperadoes of every description, and ruled by a hereditary robber chief rejoicing in the title of "King of Mud Island".' The tram journey to the Howth Road stop, a distance of about 1 km, cost one penny, rather less than the equivalent bus journey today.

There is a bus stop on the left shortly after Newcomen Bridge. From here follow Father Conmee's tram journey by bus (Nos. 24, 51 or 53), passing the 'ivy church' on the left just before the
183   railway bridge. Crossing the Tolka river by Annesley Bridge, pass Fairview Park (still to be constructed in 1904) on the right. On the left, off Fairview Strand, is Windsor Avenue, where the Joyces lived at No. 29 (one of their several Fairview addresses). Father Conmee alights at the Howth Road stop just past the Malahide Road on the left, and within view of 15 Marino Crescent, home of Bram Stoker, the author of *Dracula*.

'The Malahide road was quiet. It pleased Father Conmee, road and name.' Father Conmee walks up the Malahide Road on his way to the O'Brien Institute, an orphanage where he will arrange for Paddy Dignam's son to be admitted. While walking he thinks of 'his little book *Old Times in the Barony*', a memoir of the Athlone area which was published in 1895. The fields of the Marino estate on his left (now built over) remind him of earlier years in Co. Kildare, and he imagines himself reading his office on the Clongowes playing fields. This prompts him to reach for his breviary.

184

10. The O'Brien Institute. Father Conmee's destination is now the Dublin Fire Brigade Training Centre. On the right of the picture is the celebrated Marino Casino, now open to the public. *Lawrence Collection R 1095, courtesy of the National Library of Ireland.*

A flushed young man came from a gap of
a hedge and after him came a young woman
with wild nodding daisies in her hand. The
young man raised his cap abruptly: the young
woman abruptly bent and with slow care
detached from her light skirt a clinging twig.
Father Conmee blessed both gravely...

The young man, as we learn on page 339, is Lynch,
who turns up later in the maternity hospital.

On the left, just past Griffith Avenue, is the
O'Brien Institute, a large building set well back from
the road which now houses the Dublin Fire Brigade
Training Centre and a fire brigade museum. The
next turn to the left leads to the Marino Casino, a
gem of eighteenth-century architecture designed by
Sir William Chambers for Lord Charlemont in 1762,
restored and open to the public daily from March to
October. It is worth a visit before returning along
the North Strand Road to Amiens Street (Connolly)
Station. The No. 24 bus goes all the way from
Malahide Road near the Casino.

The station is the starting point for Tour 4.

Tour 4
Circe, Eumaeus, (Ithaca), Lotuseaters,
Wandering Rocks (xvii), Oxen of the Sun

Circe, 11.20 p.m.

350   *(The Mabbot street entrance of nighttown, before*
which stretches an uncobbled tramsiding set with skel-
eton tracks, red and green will-o'-the-wisps and danger
signals…)

The longest of all the episodes in *Ulysses*, this section is set in what was once the most notorious brothel quarter in Europe. Known at one time as 'Monto', after Montgomery Street, it was famous in its heyday for the establishments run by Mrs Mack, May Oblong and other notorious madams. It declined in later years, and one night in 1925, at the instigation of the Legion of Mary, it was thoroughly raided by the Irish police. The Legion of Mary followed in the wake of the Gardaí and took charge of the 'fallen women', many of whom were only too ready to find more respectable employment. Although most of the streets have been subjected to rebuilding and renaming, this remains one of Dublin's danger areas

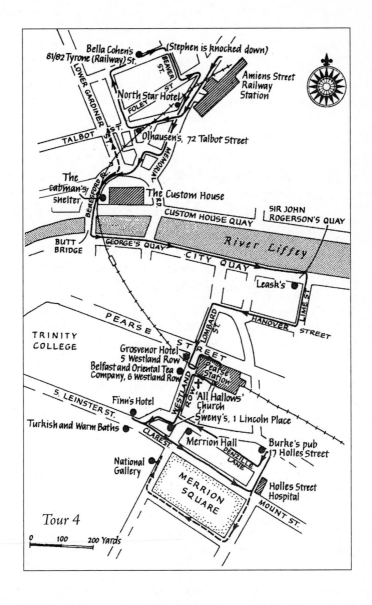

Bella Cohen's
81/82 Tyrone (Railway) St.

(Stephen is knocked down)

LOWER GARDINER ST.

BEAVER ST.

North Star Hotel

FOLEY ST.

Amiens Street
Railway
Station

TALBOT ST.

Olhausen's, 72 Talbot Street

MEMORIAL RD.

The
Cabman's
Shelter

BERESFORD PL.

The Custom House

The Custom House

CUSTOM HOUSE QUAY

SIR JOHN
ROGERSON'S QUAY

BUTT
BRIDGE

GEORGE'S QUAY

River Liffey

CITY QUAY

Leask's

LIME ST.

PEARSE

TRINITY
COLLEGE

Grosvenor Hotel
5 Westland Row
Belfast and Oriental Tea
Company, 6 Westland Row

LOMBARD ST.

HANOVER STREET

STREET

WESTLAND ROW

Pearse
Station

S. LEINSTER ST.

Finn's Hotel

'All Hallows'
Church

Sweny's, 1 Lincoln Place

Turkish and Warm Baths

CLARE ST.

Merrion Hall

DENZILLE LANE

Burke's pub
17 Holles Street

National
Gallery

MERRION
SQUARE

Holles Street
Hospital

MOUNT ST.

Tour 4

0   100   200 Yards

where street crime is common, and it should be treated with caution.

Throughout this chapter the 'real' action is confusingly mingled with hallucinations generated in the minds of Bloom and Stephen. These hallucinations represent the enchantments of the witch Circe in the original *Odyssey*, who caused Ulysses' crew to be turned into animals (a theme echoed here in the continual descriptions of humans with bestial attributes). We will thread our way through this labyrinth, distinguishing reality from hallucination.

351   Among the grotesque figures in Talbot Street loom Cissy Caffrey, apparently only a namesake of the tomboy whom we saw on Sandymount Strand, and the two English soldiers, Private Compton and Private
352 Carr. Stephen Dedalus and Lynch now appear, having taken the train from Westland Row to Amiens Street Station (now Connolly Station). They would have left the station by the side entrance beside the Loop Line
353 bridge and crossed into Talbot Street. As they proceed into Nighttown they pass 'a liver and white spaniel on the prowl'. The dog reappears constantly in the episode, as a different breed each time.

Modern-day Talbot Street has had its pavements widened and the roadway at the entrance is kinked to slow down motor traffic. On the way in to the street is a plain but imposing monument to the victims of the terrorist bomb attacks of May 1974, many of whom died here.

354   '(...*On the farther side under the railway bridge Bloom appears, flushed, panting, cramming bread and chocolate into*

a sidepocket...)' Bloom, who got on the same train as Stephen and Lynch, has got separated and has fallen behind. Precisely what happened on the journey from Holles Street is not entirely clear, but from Bloom's few comments on page 369 it can be guessed that in the confusion at Westland Row station Stephen and Lynch got into a first-class carriage with third-class tickets. Meanwhile Bloom got into a third-class carriage at the very front of the train. The engine at the back drove too far into Amiens Street station and Bloom was left for some anxious minutes with no platform to get out on, fearing that he would be taken on to Malahide or abandoned in a siding. Now, arming himself with provisions, he follows in their tracks along the south side of Talbot Street, past Gillen's at No. 64, in and out of Rabaiotti's at No. 65, and into Olhausen's at No. 72 to buy a crubeen and a sheep's trotter.

355   By Cormack's pub (now Mother Kelly's) on the corner before the lane he stops to look at the glow of a distant fire, then crosses Talbot Street after nearly colliding with two cyclists and a sandstrewer.

356 He reaches O'Beirne's pub on the diagonally opposite corner at the bottom of Mabbot Street (which later became Corporation Street and was recently, in an act of civic revenge, renamed James Joyce Street), and

357 enters Nighttown. His hallucinations begin with a

358-9 vision of his father; his mother and wife also appear.

360 He returns to reality briefly when a bawd seizes his

361-7 sleeve, but then he has visions of Gerty MacDowell and Mrs Breen, who finally fades from his side.

11. Amiens Street Station. Stephen and Lynch, and later Bloom, emerge from the suburban line station at the end of the Loop Line bridge and cross Amiens Street into Talbot Street, on the extreme left. Later on Bloom and Stephen approach down the near side of the street from beyond the bridge. *Lawrence Collection R 4067, courtesy of the National Library of Ireland.*

(…Followed by the whining dog he walks on towards hellsgates. In an archway a standing woman, bent forward, her feet apart, pisses cowily. Outside a shuttered pub a bunch of loiterers listen to a tale which their brokensnouted gaffer rasps out with raucous humour…)

Bloom's path passes Foley Street (formerly Montgomery Street) and Purdon Street. Nearby, the two redcoats and a drunken navvy are arguing with a shebeenkeeper. 'Wildgoose chase this. Disorderly houses.

368
369

Lord knows where they are gone. Drunks cover dis-
370 tance double quick.' He abandons the crubeen and
371-86 trotter to the hungry dog and drifts into another hallucination in which he is arrested, charged with a long list
387 of crimes and condemned. When the vision ends he
has taken the third turn to the right into Railway Street
(formerly Tyrone Street and Mecklenburgh Street).

> (*...All recedes. Bloom plodges forward again
> through the sump. Kisses chirp amid the rifts of
> fog. A piano sounds. He stands before a lighted
> house, listening...*).

He has reached Bella Cohen's house at No. 82, on
the left-hand side just before the convent entrance,
now fronted by a blank wall. Although it is described
in the dialogue as No. 81, the house owned for
many years by Mrs Cohen is designated in Thom's
directory as No. 82. Made legendary by *Ulysses*, she
receives no mention in anybody else's recollections,
unlike her close and infamous neighbours May

12. 88–93 Tyrone Street,
taken in 1913. Bloom
passes these houses just
before reaching Bella
Cohen's at No. 82. Like
many of the buildings in
the street, they were run
down and dilapidated.
*Reproduced by permission
of the Royal Society of
Antiquaries of Ireland ©
RSAI Lantern 7.2.*

Arnott and Annie Mack, and it is only in Joyce's novel that she is called 'Bella'. News reports and prison records (relating to her convictions for such crimes as being drunk and disorderly) suggest that her first name was Ellen and that she was about fifty-three in 1904. In the 1901 census the head of the household was forty-nine-year-old Bridget Coughlan of no stated occupation, who lived in the house with two young 'dressmakers' and a servant. Here Bloom is accosted by 'Zoe Higgins, a young
388 whore in a sapphire slip'. Stroking him, she discovers in his pocket a potato which he keeps as a good
389 luck charm, and takes it from him. Again he hal-
390-407 lucinates, becoming a popular figure, a successful national leader and a worker of miracles. Dissident voices arise and he is denounced and publicly
408 burned at the stake. Zoe invites him inside and they
409 enter the house, passing through the hall and into
410 the musicroom at the front of the building on the ground floor, where they find Stephen and Lynch
411 with two whores, Kitty and Florry. Stephen, drunk and confused, is making philosophical speeches
412 towards Lynch's cap, but is interrupted by the noise
413 of a gramophone in a nearby house. More phantom visions arise, involving the End of the World ('a two-headed octopus in gillie's kilts, busby and
414-6 tartan filibegs'), Elijah, and Stephen's listeners from
417 the library. Zoe adjusts the whistling gasjet, and
418-22 as Bloom observes her he has another hallucination, involving his grandfather Lipoti Virag and an appearance by Henry Flower.

Stephen meanwhile is still at the piano, and touches the keys. The others request a song but he declines. 'No voice. I am a most finished artist.' His mind briefly divides into 'The Siamese twins, Philip Drunk and Philip Sober.'

423 Philip Sober reminds him of all the drinking he has already done around town, in 'Mooney's en ville, Mooney's sur mer, the Moira, Larchet's, Holles Street hospital, Burke's,' but Philip Drunk continues recklessly. Florry asks him if he is out of the priests' college at Maynooth, and Zoe tells of the priest 424-7 who visited the brothel recently. The conversation continues with hallucinatory interruptions from Virag, the Philips, Henry Flower, Ben Dollard and others.

428 (*A male form passes down the creaking staircase and is heard taking the waterproof and hat from the rack. Bloom starts forward involuntarily and, half closing the door as he passes, takes the chocolate from his pocket and offers it nervously to Zoe.*)

429 Bloom speculates that the man in the hall is Boylan but relaxes when he hears a 'male cough and tread… passing through the mist outside.'

430 Bella Cohen, the whoremistress, now enters the 431-43 room. Bloom, awed by her dominating appearance, plunges into a long and harrowing hallucination in which Bella becomes a man and he himself becomes a woman. He is mistreated, dressed up, humiliated, put to work in the brothel and auctioned to the

444   highest bidder. In the depths of his shame he is
       confronted by the nymph from the *Photo Bits* print
445-9 in his bedroom, who reproaches him with his secret
450   lusts and masturbations. Through his fantasies leak
       sounds from the real world as Kitty asks Florry for a
       cushion. Reality comes closer when his back trouser
       button snaps, breaking the spell.

451   Suddenly restored to an awareness of his own
       virility, Bloom gains confidence. The nymph flees, and
452   a moment later he is able to return the stare of the
       awesome Mrs Cohen with composure and contempt.
453   This is a turning point for him. Bloom gains further
       ground by reclaiming his potato from Zoe, and
       Bella descends on the swaying Stephen for payment.
454   Confused by drink, he hands her a poundnote, a
       gold half sovereign and two crowns – a total of two
       pounds, or ten shillings too much since the rate is ten
455   shillings a girl. Bloom insists on paying for himself,
       and prevents Stephen being cheated.

BLOOM
*(quietly lays a half sovereign on the table between
Bella and Florry)* So. Allow me. *(he takes up the
poundnote)* Three times ten. We're square.

He returns the pound to Stephen, who drops a box
of matches and is still witty enough to make a remark
456   about falling Lucifers. Bloom offers to take care of
       Stephen's money before he loses any more.
457-9   Zoe reads Stephen's and Bloom's palms, and sees in
       Bloom's hand something which causes her to whisper
       and giggle with Florry and the others. Excluded from

460-2   the joke, he slips into fantasy, imagining Boylan's visit to Molly with himself as a compliant and ridiculous

463   cuckold. Stephen and Bloom gaze together into the mirror and Shakespeare's face appears, horned and

464   uttering incoherent quotations. The whores persuade

465   Stephen to 'give us some parleyvoo' and he delivers a recital in broken English promoting some of the

466   seamier entertainments of Paris. He tells them of his dream of the previous night – 'I flew. My foes beneath

467   me' – and in a fantasy he sees himself as a fox, running from the hounds. The hunt turns into a horserace with Mr Deasy bringing up the rear.

468   '(*Private Carr, Private Compton and Cissy Caffrey pass beneath the windows, singing in discord.*)' On cue, Stephen is reminded of the definition of God which he gave Mr Deasy – 'Our friend noise in the street.' The song they are singing is 'My Girl's a Yorkshire Girl' and Zoe

469-71   sets the pianola going with the same tune. Stephen starts dancing with all the girls, surrounded by fantasy figures including the music and dancing masters Professor Goodwin and Professor Maginni. The

472   others form couples and he continues dancing wildly on his own, whirling giddily till the music ends and he

473   stops dead. A horrible vision now confronts him – his mother, rising through the floor, her body dead and rotting. Buck Mulligan, who earlier accused Stephen of killing his mother, appears in the background to

474   reinforce her reproaches. The others only see that

475   Stephen has gone white, and Florry goes to get him some water. Stephen refuses to let his spirit be broken, and lashes out in rage.

(*…He lifts his ashplant high with both hands and smashes the chandelier. Time's livid final flame leaps and, in the following darkness, ruin of all space, shattered glass and toppling masonry*).

476 He dashes from the house, and the others rush towards the hall door. Bella seizes Bloom's coattail and demands ten shillings for the broken lamp.

477 'There's not sixpenceworth of damage done,' retorts Bloom, throwing down a shilling and hurrying to

478 the door. On the doorstep the whores are pointing at a disturbance down the street, and a hackney car arrives outside bearing Corny Kelleher and 'two silent lechers'. Bloom hastens past them and turns left along the street, seeing in his imagination a great crowd rushing after him with hue and cry.

479 '(*At the corner of Beaver street beneath the scaffolding Bloom panting stops on the fringe of the noisy quarrelling knot…*)' Stephen, it appears, has addressed or accosted Cissy Caffrey while the soldiers were relieving themselves, and a row has developed.

480 Private Compton is urging Private Carr to hit Stephen. (Carr, incidentally, derived his name from a British consular official in Zurich, Henry Carr, with whom Joyce had a particularly ludicrous dispute in 1917. The incident formed the basis for Tom Stoppard's play *Travesties*.)

481 Bloom tries to pull Stephen away, but without success. Stephen, still rebellious against any attempt to master him, especially by his arch-enemies the Church and the State, makes a rambling reference

to killing 'the priest and the king'. Carr seizes on this
482   as an insulting reference to King Edward VII, who
immediately materialises, wearing a white jersey and
483   sucking a red jujube. Bloom tries desperately to calm
484   the soldiers and remove Stephen, but the argument
485   escalates, attended by the imaginary figure of 'Old
Gummy Granny' (a grotesque version of Kathleen Ni
Houlihan), symbolising the Irish nationalist cause. All
this is lacking now is the third of Stephen's would-be-
486   masters, the Church. 'How do I stand you? The hat
trick! Where's the third person of the Blessed Trinity?
487-9 Soggarth Aroon? The reverend Carrion Crow.' This
body is duly represented by Father Malachi O'Flynn and
the Reverend Mr Hugh C. Haines Love, MA (Mulligan
and Haines in disguise, it would seem) celebrating a
black Mass.

490   Lynch, who has been watching with Kitty, sneaks off,
491   and while Bloom still tries to calm things down, Private
Carr rushes forward, strikes Stephen and knocks him
out. The lurking dog, now identified as a retriever, barks
492   furiously, and two policemen turn up. Private Compton
pulls Carr away, and Bloom is trying to explain matters
493   to the police when Corny Kelleher appears. Knowing
Kelleher's influence with the police, Bloom enlists his help
494   in getting them to disperse the crowd and leave Stephen
495   alone. The policemen leave, followed by Kelleher on his
496   outside car, and Bloom stands by Stephen as he gradually
497   comes to. His last hallucination is of his dead son Rudy.
'...*a fairy boy of eleven, a changeling, kidnapped, dressed in an
Eton suit with glass shoes and a little bronze helmet, holding a book
in his hand.*'

Eumaeus, 12.40 a.m.

501   Preparatory to anything else Mr Bloom
brushed off the greater bulk of the shavings
and handed Stephen the hat and ashplant
and bucked him up generally in orthodox
Samaritan fashion which he very badly needed.

The new chapter begins where *Circe* ended, at the corner of Railway Street and Beaver Street. Fitting to the
condition of the protagonists, the style is weary and
clumsy, full of mixed metaphors, worn clichés and
stumbling syntax. The first priority is refreshment.

Accordingly [...] they both walked together
along Beaver street or, more properly, lane
as far as the farrier's and the distinctly fetid
atmosphere of the livery stables at the corner
of Montgomery street where they made
tracks to the left from thence debouching into
Amiens street round by the corner of Dan
Bergin's.

Montgomery Street, now Foley Street, still retains
its cobbles, but the malodorous stables have given
way to modern apartments. Dan Bergin's pub is now
Lloyd's. Many of the establishments which they pass
can easily be identified: Mullett's name is still over his
back door on Foley Street, though the pub has gone,
the North Star Hotel still flourishes, the Signal House
is now Cleary's and Amiens Street railway terminus is,
of course, Connolly Station.

502   They passed the main entrance of the Great Northern railway station, […] and passing the backdoor of the morgue (a not very enticing locality, not to say gruesome to a degree, more especially at night) ultimately gained the Dock Tavern and in due course turned into Store Street, famous for its C division police station.

The Dock Tavern, next door to the morgue, has now been redesigned and bears the name of The Bow Dock, and the police are still in residence 503 in a revamped office nearby. Passing what is now the central bus station (one of Dublin's first public buildings in the modern style, designed in 1953 by Michael Scott), 'they made a beeline across the back of the Customhouse and passed under the Loop Line bridge'.

In one line Joyce mentions one of Dublin's most handsome constructions and one of its most abominable eyesores. The Custom House, designed by James Gandon and built 1781–91, appears at its most impressive from the far side of the river. Gutted by fire during the Troubles in 1921, the building has since been painstakingly and beautifully restored, with the replacement of much of the stonework. The Loop Line bridge was built in 1891 to connect the stations in Westland Row and Amiens Street and is constantly denounced for its impact on the view of the Custom House. The 'beeline' made by our two heroes across Beresford Place, rather dubious from the first, is now a suicidal impossibility due to the convergence of

13. Beresford Place, on the occasion of the arrest of Count Plunkett at a protest meeting in 1919. At the centre stands the cabman's shelter, with the bearded Count visible above the crowd nearby, and the corner of the Custom House behind the railway bridge. *Keogh Collection KE 176, courtesy of the National Library of Ireland.*

traffic from several different directions, and a patient use of pedestrian lights is advised.

504   Under the bridge, where Eamonn O'Doherty's statue of James Connolly now stands facing the site of his headquarters at Liberty Hall, Stephen is hailed by an acquaintance, 'Lord' John Corley (who appears in *Dubliners* as Lenehan's companion in 'Two Gallants'). Corley is down on his luck and asks Stephen to lend

505   him some money. Stephen, who despite Bloom's concern did not hand over all his money to his care, discovers that he has some halfcrowns in his pocket which he mistakes for pennies (the coins were similar in size though not in metal).

506   Bloom continues on his way with Stephen, attempting to give him some advice about his choice
507 of friends, especially after the scene at Westland Row Station where Mulligan and Haines apparently made it obvious that they did not want Stephen to come back to the Tower.

508   'Mr Bloom and Stephen entered the cabman's shelter, an unpretentious wooden structure...' The shelter stood beside the railway bridge near the south-west corner of the Custom House. The plaque erected in 2004 to mark the spot is slightly misplaced and should be on the next pier nearer the river. Here Bloom orders coffee and a bun and they study the other occupants of the shelter, including its keeper, who may or may not be the celebrated Invincible, Fitzharris, known as Skin-the-Goat.

509   In keeping with the original episode in the *Odyssey*, where Ulysses appears in disguise, there are continual references in this episode to mistaken and dubious identities, confused and disguised names and unreliable stories. It begins with the redbearded sailor who asks Stephen's name and claims to know a Simon Dedalus
510 who turns out to be a circus sharpshooter. The sailor's name is D. B. Murphy; by an appropriate chance this appeared as W. B. Murphy until the Corrected Text
511 proposed a new identity for him. The picture postcard
512 which he produces is addressed, however, to Señor A.
513 Boudin. He is full of colourful tales, about the Chinese
514 with his little pills and the stabbing incident in Trieste,
515-16 but is elusive when questioned. Even the man's face tattooed on his chest is capable of being changed.

517   Bloom is distracted from this entertaining spectacle
by the sight of a streetwalker looking in through the
door – the same one whom he saw earlier on Ormond
Quay and by whom he is scared of being recognised. He
converses with Stephen about the evils of prostitution

518 and then asks him 'as a good catholic' about his views
on the soul. Stephen's reply leaves Bloom a bit out of
his depth and he ventures instead to persuade Stephen

519 to tackle the coffee and bun. Their attention returns

520 to the sailor and his scarcely credible yarns, which are

521-2 interrupted when the mariner goes outside to 'unfurl
a reef'. The men's urinal, to which he is directed and
where the others observed the Italians earlier, was
probably at the corner of the bridge with Eden Quay –
too far for the sailor to bother availing of it.

523-4   The conversation in the shelter turns to the
subject of Irish Home Rule and an argument begins

525 between the sailor and the keeper. Bloom takes up the
subject with Stephen and tells him about the incident

526 in Barney Kiernan's. Their views on nationality and

527 nationalism differ, and Stephen gets crosstempered,
saying: '—We can't change the country. Let us change
the subject.'

528   Bloom picks up a nearby copy of 'the pink edition
extra sporting of the *Telegraph* tell a graphic lie' in
which he is momentarily jolted by misreading 'Hugh

529 Boylan' for H. du Boyes, and reads Hynes's report on
the Dignam funeral, which contains his own name,
misspelt, and those of others who were not even
there. Bloom is 'Nettled not a little by L. Boom (as
it incorrectly stated) and the line of bitched type

but tickled to death simultaneously by C. P. M'Coy and Stephen Dedalus B.A. who were conspicuous, needless to say, by their total absence (to say nothing of M'Intosh) …' The paper also contains Mr Deasy's letter and an account of the Gold Cup race.

530 The others in the shelter begin a conversation
531 about Parnell, the possibility of his not being dead
532 after all, and Kitty O'Shea, who Bloom recalls had
533 Spanish blood. This prompts him to show Stephen
534-5 a photograph of Molly which Stephen politely
admires. Bloom thinks it a pity that Stephen should be
536 wasting his time with 'profligate women' and, further
solicitous for his welfare, asks him 'At what o'clock
did you dine?'

—Some time yesterday, Stephen said.
—Yesterday! exclaimed Bloom till he remembered it was already tomorrow Friday. Ah, you mean it's after twelve!
—The day before yesterday, Stephen said, improving on himself.

537 Bloom decides to offer Stephen 'a cup of Epps's cocoa
538-9 and a shakedown for the night'. He pays the fourpenny
bill and supports Stephen outside. Chatting about
music, 'they made tracks arm in arm across Beresford
540 place', rounding the back of the Custom House inside
the 'swingchains' at the edge of the road. Nearby, a
horse, dragging a sweeper, is being used to clean the
541 street after the horse traffic of the day. They stop as
it crosses their path. Stephen, showing signs of recov-
542 ery, is illustrating the conversation by singing; Bloom

543 admires Stephen's voice and considers advising him to concentrate seriously on a singing career. They take advantage of a pause when the horse stops to let fall 'three smoking globes of turds', and cross the wide roadway towards Gardiner Street Lower. The driver watches them as they disappear up the street in the direction of Bloom's house.

Ithaca, 1 a.m.

The route from here to Bloom's house is described in Tour 3 and connects with it. To continue this tour, cross Butt Bridge and turn left along George's Quay and City Quay, following the route presumably taken by Bloom between *Calypso* and *Lotuseaters*.

Lotuseaters, 9.45 a.m.

58   By lorries along sir John Rogerson's quay Mr Bloom walked soberly, past Windmill lane, Leask's the linseed crusher, the postal telegraph office.

Bloom's unnecessarily circuitous route from home takes him well down the quays, then busy with maritime traffic. The Loop Line was at that time Dublin's easternmost bridge, since enclosed by the Matt Talbot Bridge, the Seán O'Casey Bridge for pedestrians, the striking Samuel Beckett Bridge designed by Santiago Calatrava, and the East Link Bridge further down. No longer

14. Eden Quay and Butt Bridge. The clock on the left belongs to 'Mooney's *sur mer*'. The centre section of Butt Bridge, in the middle of the picture, is mounted on a turntable. *Lawrence Collection I 2293, courtesy of the National Library of Ireland.*

alive with dockers and seamen, Sir John Rogerson's Quay is now a pretty promenade. Bloom's way leads past Windmill Lane, now famous for its recording studios where Irish rock legends U2 made their way into history. A proliferation of tribute graffiti on the studio wall and surroundings led to the erection of a plaintive sign on the neighbouring building to announce 'This is not The Wall' and directing them next door to the appropriate area. Bloom passes Leask's, now the Columbia Bar and Grill, the post office next door and the sailors' home on the corner of Lime Street,

15. Brady's Cottages, taken in 1913. A rare glimpse in *Ulysses* into one of the poorer areas in Dublin. *Reproduced by permission of the Royal Society of Antiquaries of Ireland © RSAI Lantern 7.29.*

where he turns right, away from the quayside. Brady's Cottages, on either side of Lime Street, are long since demolished, and the new apartment complex fails to match the squalid atmosphere conveyed by Joyce. He turns right along Hanover Street and into Townsend Street, which he crosses to turn left up Lombard Street. 'Bethel', the Salvation Army hall on the right, has gone, but Nichols' the undertaker still flourishes on the same side. Joyce House, home of the General Register Office opposite Nichols', is connected with the author of *Ulysses* only in name.

Crossing Great Brunswick Street (now Pearse Street), he goes up the right hand side of Westland Row and halts just beyond the railway bridge before the window of the Belfast and Oriental Tea Company (where the railings of the O'Reilly Institute now stand). Finally, holding a *Freeman's*

59

Journal which he has bought on the way from Eccles Street, he crosses to the post office, which was situated beneath the bridge inside where the station entrance is now, and collects a letter addressed to 'Henry Flower Esq'.

60   Strolling out of the post office and turning to the right, he encounters M'Coy, and gazes idly past him during the conversation at the woman entering the carriage outside the Grosvenor Hotel, which stood next to the railway bridge across the street from the station. Conway's pub, to which M'Coy refers, is now

61   Kennedy's on the corner of Lincoln Place. Eluding
62   M'Coy at last, Bloom strolls on towards Brunswick Street.

> Wonder is he pimping after me?
> Mr Bloom stood at the corner, his eyes wandering over the multicoloured hoardings. Cantrell and Cochrane's Ginger Ale (Aromatic). Clery's Summer Sale. No, he's going on straight.

63   He turns right onto Brunswick Street, where the wall covered with hoardings has been replaced by a large student accommodation block (connected to the Trinity College campus by its own footbridge across Westland Row). The 'hazard' still serves as a taxi rank, but the cabhorses and the shelter are gone. 'He turned into Cumberland street and, going on some paces, halted in the lee of the station wall. No-one.'

    Here in private he opens the letter. It is from Martha
64   Clifford, whom he has never met and with whom he is carrying on a clandestine erotic correspondence.

65   He tears up the envelope under the railway arch, and reaches 'the open backdoor of All Hallows' on the right beyond the lane. This door, and the gateway to the side lane, are rarely left open nowadays, and it may be necessary to retrace the route back into Westland Row, past the station, and into the church by the front door to pick up Bloom's trail inside. Officially St Andrew's (by James Boulger, 1832–7) the church was also known locally as All Hallows, perhaps with some connection to the ancient monastery of that name which stood on the grounds now occupied by Trinity College.

16. St Andrew's Church. Called 'All Hallows' by Joyce, the church has changed little since Bloom emerged and turned left towards Sweny's. *Lawrence Collection R 1197, courtesy of the National Library of Ireland.*

66   Entering the church, Bloom finds communion in progress and takes a quiet seat in the corner, observing
67   the proceedings. The original of this episode in the *Odyssey* described the Lotus Eaters, a hopelessly
68   addicted band of dropouts; and the so-called 'opiate of the people' becomes the subject of Bloom's thoughts here. He decides to leave before they come round with the plate, and emerges by the front door into Westland Row, next to the post office. Outside, he turns left.

'Sweny's in Lincoln place. Chemists rarely move.' The 'green and gold beaconjars' have gone, but Sweny's is still there in Lincoln Place, at the far end of Westland Row, complete with its original nameplate, shop-front and interior furnishings. The pharmacy closed in 2008 and was reopened to be run by a voluntary group who sell second-hand books, postcards, non-prescription medicines and, of course, lemon soap for the many imitators of Bloom who call
69   in. The real purpose of Bloom's visit is to get some lotion made up for Molly; he arranges to call back later in the day but eventually omits to do so.

70   Outside Sweny's, Bloom is accosted by Bantam Lyons, who has probably spotted him from inside Conway's. Lyons borrows Bloom's paper to look up the Ascot runners, and Bloom gets impatient. He tells Lyons he can keep the paper.

—I was just going to throw it away, Mr Bloom said.

   Bantam Lyons raised his eyes suddenly and leered weakly.

—What's that? his sharp voice said.

—I say you can keep it, Mr Bloom answered. I was going to throw it away that moment.

Bantam Lyons doubted an instant, leering: then thrust the outspread sheets back on Mr Bloom's arms.

—I'll risk it, he said. Here, thanks.

Bloom thus unwittingly gives a tip for the eventual winner of the Gold Cup, Throwaway.

Turning left, he walks 'cheerfully towards the mosque of the baths'. The Lincoln Place Baths, on the site now occupied by the Lincoln House building, were designed in Oriental style by Richard Barter in 1859. However, this establishment, which had closed in 1899, was not the one where Bloom goes for his bath. We discover elsewhere in the book that he went further on to the Turkish and Warm Baths, 11 Leinster Street. On the other side of Lincoln Place he observes Hornblower the college porter standing outside his lodge (an attractive stone structure which was taken down in 2001 to make way for another building) inside the back gate of Trinity College.

71 Continue along Lincoln Place into South Leinster Street. The last building on the right before the College railings was once Finn's Hotel, where Joyce's wife Nora Barnacle worked as a chambermaid. The name may still be seen in faded white paint on the gable wall. Nearly opposite Finn's an office block at No. 11 now occupies the site of the baths where Bloom foresees himself.

He saw his trunk and limbs riprippled over and sustained, buoyed lightly upward, lemonyellow: his navel, bud of flesh: and saw the dark tangled curls of his bush floating, floating hair of the stream around the limp father of thousands, a languid floating flower.

After his bath, Bloom takes the tram to Sandymount for the funeral.

Wandering Rocks xvii

205   Almidano Artifoni walked past Holles street, past Sewell's yard. Behind him Cashel Boyle O'Connor Fitzmaurice Tisdall Farrell, with stickumbrelladustcoat dangling, shunned the lamp before Mr Law Smith's house and crossing, walked along Merrion square. Distantly behind him a blind stripling tapped his way by the wall of College park.

Artifoni, having missed the tram outside Trinity, is walking to Ballsbridge. Farrell is on his way from the National Library, where he was signing the reader's book on page 177. On page 201 he was seen passing the Kildare Street club as he turned the corner into Nassau Street. The blind stripling, whom Bloom saw about two hours previously approaching Levenston's Dancing Academy in South Frederick Street, has since been up to the Ormond Hotel to tune the piano. Shortly after we see him here he will realise that he has left his tuningfork behind, and will go all the way back to retrieve it.

Farrell walks all the way to the corner of Holles Street, then turns and retraces his steps so that when the viceroy passes he is outside Finn's Hotel, staring at the head of Maurice Solomons in his optician's shop where he also served as the Austro-Hungarian viceconsul (page 208). The shop, at 19 Nassau Street, just beyond the Dawson Street corner, cannot in fact have been easily visible from here.

From Finn's Hotel (opposite the entrance to the Millennium Wing of the National Gallery of Ireland) walk along Clare Street and Merrion Square North, passing the landmarks of Farrell's walk in reverse order. 'Mr Bloom's dental windows' were at 2 Clare Street, where Marcus Bloom had his practice, and Law Smith's house was on the next corner. Between them at No. 6 were the offices of Beckett and Medcalf, where Samuel Beckett lived in the 1930s above the family firm and wrote his early novels. Across the next street, on the corner of Merrion Square, was the former residence of Sir William Wilde and the childhood home of his famous son Oscar (who is commemorated by an unusual statue inside the railings of the green opposite). It was outside this house that James Joyce had his first rendezvous with Nora Barnacle on 14 June 1904. She stood him up. Halting at this corner, Farrell frowns northwards at the notice on Merrion Hall (now the Davenport Hotel), and southwards at 'the distant pleasance of duke's lawn' outside Leinster House (just beyond the other entrance to the National Gallery on Merrion Street). 'Mr Lewis Werner's cheerful windows', on the corner house at the far end of Merrion Square North, are now preserved in the Kenny Gallery in Galway.

From here cross the street to the Maternity Hospital. The entrance is halfway down Holles Street, and a plaque there commemorating its connection with *Ulysses* will hopefully remain when the hospital itself moves operations south of the city by 2018.

Oxen of the Sun, 10 p.m.

314   Deshil Holles Eamus. Deshil Holles Eamus. Deshil Holles Eamus.

The National Maternity Hospital in Holles Street was opened in 1894, under the mastership of Dr Andrew Horne. Major rebuilding was carried out in 1934, including the neo-Georgian façade of the Nurses' Residence on the Merrion Square side. The Holles Street front was not greatly altered in style. The precise location of the common room inside the building, where most of the events take place, is not clear.

The form of this episode was based by Joyce on the growth of the baby in the womb, from conception to birth. The language of the episode evolves historically as it goes along, beginning with primitive incantations, proceeding with what look like word for word translations from Greek and Latin and so through old and Middle English to a brilliant series of pastiches on the styles of the major writers in English literature, century by century.

315   After a short introduction dealing with fertility, childbirth, medicine and maternity care, Bloom makes his appearance. 'Some man that wayfaring was stood by housedoor at night's oncoming. Of Israel's folk was that man that on earth wandering far had fared.' Bloom has arrived by tram from Sandymount, and has come to visit his friend Mrs Purefoy.

316   Lightning flashes as the nurse at the door, crossing herself, lets him in. She is Nurse Callan, who rented out a flat in Holles Street to the Blooms during their hard times some years previously. Bloom learns from her of the death of a young medical friend, Doctor

17. Holles Street Hospital in the early years of the century. Bloom enters by the 'housedoor' beside the sign. *Courtesy of the National Maternity Hospital.*

O'Hare. He asks after Mrs Purefoy and learns that her long labour is nearly over.

317   Just then a medical student named Dixon, who treated Bloom for a bee sting on Whit Monday at the Mater Misericordiae Hospital, appears and invites Bloom to join his colleagues and himself for a drink inside. Bloom is reluctantly persuaded to sit down and take his hat off, though he takes care to drink little,

318   unlike the rest of the company. Besides Dixon and four other students he finds Lenehan and Stephen Dedalus, who has been drinking all afternoon, all awaiting the arrival of Buck Mulligan.

Oxen of the Sun parallels an episode in the *Odyssey* in which Ulysses' crew kill and eat oxen sacred to Apollo. The students, too, show little respect for the sacred cows of medical ethics, and embark on a

319   jocular discussion of whether to save the mother or the child in a birth where it is a case of one life or the

320   other. Bloom is painfully reminded of the death of his baby son Rudy.

Stephen meanwhile, merry with drink, fills all the glasses and shows off some money which he claims to have received 'for a song which he writ', though in fact it appears to be the remains of the morning's pay from Mr Deasy, depleted by thirteen shillings which would seem to have been spent on drink for himself and others. Ready to show that for him especially nothing is sacred, he poses a theosophical conundrum to prove that whether Mary conceived Jesus wittingly or unwittingly, there is nothing special in her by

321   herself to be venerated. Punch Costello, one of the

students, starts up a bawdy song but is silenced first by Nurse Quigley and then by his colleagues.

322   Tales of Stephen's womanising are told, while he himself reflects on his treatment by Mulligan which symbolises his treatment by Ireland as a whole: 'Remember, Erin, […] how thou settedst little by me and by my word and broughtedst in a stranger to my gates […] and hast made me, thy lord, to be the slave of servants […]. Why hast thou done this abomination before me that thou didst spurn me for a merchant

323 of jalaps…?' Even as he jeers at the futility of any attempt to relate our life to any sort of immortality, the thunderstorm breaks over them. 'A black crack of noise in the street here, alack, bawled back. Loud on left Thor thundered: in anger awful the hammerhurler.'

    Stephen, interpreting the 'noise in the street' as the voice of an angry God, is frightened, despite Bloom's

324 assurance that it can all be explained scientifically. A pastiche of *The Pilgrim's Progress* tells how Stephen and his fellows are less interested in godliness than in whoring, protected by 'a stout shield of oxengut and […] they might take no hurt neither from Offspring that was that wicked devil by virtue of this same shield which was named Killchild'. Condoms are another desecration of this building devoted to the bringing forth of children.

325   Outside, as rain pours down on Dublin, Buck Mulligan, on his way from George Moore's in Ely Place, meets Alec Bannon outside Justice Fitzgibbon's at 10 Merrion Square North and invites him to come with

326 him to the hospital. Meanwhile a discussion has begun

about the foot-and-mouth disease (the slaughter of
327 oxen again being relevant here), from which arises the
tale of the two bulls, a fable about the two churches
in Ireland. The first is the Roman Catholic Church,
which arrived in Ireland in 1170 when the English
pope Adrian IV (Nicholas Breakspear or 'farmer
Nicholas') gave his blessing to Henry II's conquest
328 of Ireland with his papal bull *Laudabiliter*. The second
is the Church of England, founded with Henry VIII
('the Lord Harry') as its head.

Mulligan and Bannon now arrive, and Mulligan
329 proposes his scheme to buy Lambay Island off the
north Dublin coast and set himself up as a stud farm.
330 Bannon meanwhile accepts a drink from Crotthers, the
331 Scottish student, and displays to him a locket with a
picture of his girlfriend (Milly Bloom, as it happens).
The conversation once again turns to condoms – 'But at
this point a bell tinkling in the hall cut short a discourse
which promised so bravely for the enrichment of our
store of knowledge.'

332 Nurse Callan enters to inform Dixon that Mrs
Purefoy's labour is over and that the baby is a boy.
Punch Costello makes ribald remarks about the nurse
as soon as her back is turned, but he is rebuked by
333-4 Dixon, who goes to attend to his duties. Mr Bloom
rejoices at the news but the others are less respectful
335 in their comments. They burst forth in a discussion of
every type of abnormal birth from the commonplace
336 Caesarean section to monstrous and deformed births.
Mulligan then conjures up for them a ludicrous vision
of Haines, who, it seems, made a brief appearance

337   at the soirée in Ely Place, witnessed by Moore ('the dissipated host') and Russell ('the seer'), to tell Mulligan, 'Meet me at Westland Row station at ten past eleven.'

338   Bloom meanwhile is in a daydream about his youth, and then appears to nod off into a strange dream about a moving herd of beasts, about his daughter Milly and a mysterious writing which transforms itself into 'Alpha, a ruby and triangled sign upon the forehead of Taurus.'

339   Around him the others are discussing old times in Clongowes, the horse race, and Lynch's encounter with
340   Father Conmee that afternoon. Lenehan, reaching for a bottle of Bass, is restrained by Mulligan, who indicates Bloom's dreamy gaze fixed on the red triangle on the label. Bloom comes to and pours Lenehan some ale.
341   The conversation continues and they discuss such matters as the future determination of sex and, to a
342   greater length, infant mortality.

343   'Meanwhile the skill and patience of the physician
344   had brought about a happy *accouchement*.' The birth is over and Bloom is observing Stephen, remembering the occasion when he met him as a child at Matt
345   Dillon's. Suddenly – 'Burke's! outflings my lord Stephen, giving the cry, and a tag and bobtail of all them after…'

   The revellers burst out of the hospital and turn
346   right, heading for the pub at the bottom of the street. 'Jay, look at the drunken minister coming out of the maternity hospital!' remark the boys in Denzille Lane across the street, deceived by Stephen's 'Latin quarter

hat'. They reach Burke's on the corner of Holles Street and Denzille (now Fenian) Street at ten to eleven. (The pub has been demolished and the site is occupied by a modern block). Stephen orders the drinks – absinthe for himself, ginger cordial for Bloom, and five pints of Bass's No. 1 Ale and two pints of Guinness among 347 the others. Snatches of conversation are heard: Dixon telling someone about Bloom, Mulligan remarking that Stephen's telegram message of the morning was 'Cribbed out of Meredith'; and Stephen, the known possessor of money, being encouraged by his comrades to pay the barman for the entire round of drinks at a cost of 'Two bar and a wing' (two shillings and sixpence). Someone, possibly Lenehan, sees Bantam Lyons drowning his sorrows in the pub.

348 'You move a motion? Steve boy, you're going it some. More bluggy drunkables?' Stephen orders another round as closing time is called – absinthe all round, except for Bloom, who has a glass of wine. Bannon overhears Bloom's name and realises 'Photo's papli, by all that's gorgeous.' Mulligan has slipped away to the station. The mystery man in the macintosh is noticed; apparently he is known as Bartle the Bread and has seen better days.

349 As they leave the pub Stephen and Lynch slip off up Holles Street and along Denzille Lane, trailed by Bloom, and emerge from the lane by Merrion Hall with its notice 'Elijah is coming! Washed in the blood of the Lamb.' Long known as a gospel hall, the building is now the Davenport Hotel. From Lincoln Place they proceed down Westland Row to

the station, on their way to 'the kips where shady Mary is'.

From Pearse Station you may take the train to Sandymount for Tour 2a or Sandycove for Tour 1.

Alternatively, from Holles Street return round the east, south and west sides of Merrion Square, passing the houses of Daniel O'Connell (No. 58), W. B. Yeats (Nos. 52 and 82), Sheridan Le Fanu (No. 70) and George Russell (A.E.) (No. 84), Leinster House, and the National Gallery of Ireland, which has portraits of Joyce by Sean O'Sullivan, Wyndham Lewis, Frank Budgen and Jacques-Emile Blanche.

Tour 5

Wandering Rocks (xv, ix, xvi, x, xiii, xi, xiv, viii), Sirens

Wandering Rocks xv

202   —The youngster will be all right, Martin Cunningham said, as they passed out of the Castleyard gate.

Before setting out on this tour, it is worth visiting Dublin Castle, one of the city's most historic buildings, originally constructed in the early thirteenth century. Parts of it, including the spectacular Chester Beatty Library and the State Apartments, are open to the public when not in use for state functions.

Cunningham, Mr Power and John Wyse Nolan emerge from the upper Castleyard gate, uphill from City Hall, with the list of subscriptions collected for Paddy Dignam's family. They pass City Hall (another impressive public building) and walk down Cork Hill into Parliament Street, meeting Jimmy Henry on the way.

Passing the watchmaker's at 30 Parliament Street, 203 they turn the corner into Essex Gate and meet long

18. City Hall. Martin Cunningham, Mr Power and John Wyse Nolan come out of the Upper Castleyard gate, on the extreme right of the picture, and walk across Cork Hill, on the left, passing the councillors on the steps of City Hall. *Lawrence Collection R 1650, courtesy of the National Library of Ireland.*

John Fanning in the doorway of James Kavanagh's winerooms. Thoroughly revamped in recent years, the premises are now described as 'The Turk's Head Chop House'. The doorway, which formerly led to a stairway and an upstairs lounge, is now an emergency exit and the stairs have gone. As they all go in and upstairs, John Wyse Nolan watches the viceregal cavalcade riding past up Parliament Street. In interpolations we see the barmaids looking out of the Ormond Hotel window, and Blazes Boylan meeting Bob Doran in Grafton Street.

From the Turk's Head, cross Parliament Street to Essex Street, entering the celebrated Temple Bar area

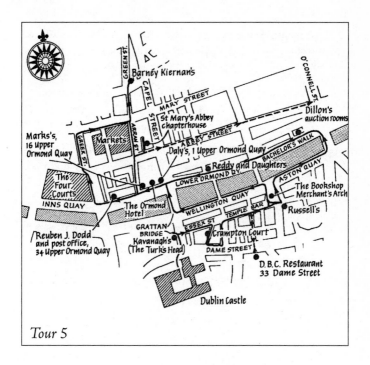

Tour 5

of the city, of which there is a map on the wall to the right. Take the second turn to the right into the laneway which leads to Crampton Court, beside the Olympia Theatre. Built about 1740 by Philip Crampton, the little courtyard with its arched entrance still exists but the west and north sides have been rebuilt in recent years.

Wandering Rocks ix

191   Tom Rochford took the top disk from the pile he clasped against his claret waistcoat.

It is not clear whether this exchange takes place inside Dan Lowry's Empire Musichall (now the Olympia Theatre), or outside the side door in the corner of the courtyard. Tom Rochford is demonstrating to Lenehan, M'Coy and Nosey Flynn his invention for showing what turn is on – presumably in the musichall programme. Lenehan is to canvass Boylan's support for the device. As Eamonn Finn recently discovered, the invention was a real one, involving a contraption mounted at the side of the stage with a series of numbered discs corresponding to items in the programme and enabling latecomers to see at a glance what items they had missed and what was now running. A full description, with Rochford's drawings, was published in *The James Joyce Broadsheet*.

Lenehan, who was last seen heading for Mooney's with Stephen, is now bound for another drink in the Ormond Hotel. He and M'Coy leave Crampton Court by the exit into Dame Street, turning left past the theatre and left again down Sycamore Street, past the stage door. The rescue from the sewer which Lenehan describes was a real event, which did not in fact take place until 6 May 1905 and which is commemorated by a monument on the site in Hawkins Street next to Burgh Quay. Rochford was only one of several people who were involved, including Constable Sheahan who died in the rescue attempt. Lenehan and M'Coy emerge next to the east corner of the Dolphin Hotel (now occupied by The Snug public house; but the west end has been preserved, complete with its carved dolphin, as an office building). Just to their right is

19. Eustace Street. Marcus Tertius Moses' office is on the right, with the triangular pediment over the door. The pub on the corner, Mullally Bros., was O'Neill's in 1904. *Lawrence Collection R 5941, courtesy of the National Library of Ireland.*

now the National Photographic Archive, a section of the National Library of Ireland, which was the source for most of the photographs in this book.

They turn right along Essex Street, pausing at the bottom of Eustace Street to check the time in 'Marcus Tertius Moses' sombre office' – now Bruno's less sombre restaurant – and O'Neill's pub (now The Norseman). In the *Dubliners* story 'Counterparts', O'Neill's is the pub visited by Farrington, who slips out of Crosbie and Alleyne's office up the street in the middle of the day for a quick drink. It was renamed Farrington's for a few years recently until, presumably, the owners wished to disassociate their premises from a drunk and child-beater. St Winifred's Well, outside the pub, was unknown to Dubliners of 1904 and only rediscovered in the late twentieth century.

The Temple Bar area, through which they are walking, has undergone a remarkable transformation since the early 1990s. A maze of narrow streets originally scheduled for demolition in an urban transport scheme, it bred a bohemian culture of arts centres, restaurants and second-hand shops. When the scheme was dropped the tenants stayed on to become the vital ingredient in a new revitalised cultural quarter. It is a strange mixture of genuinely historical streets and buildings, exciting new architecture, outdoor art, cultural centres and more than enough 'fashionable' pubs and restaurants.

192   In Temple Bar (the central street which has since given its name to the whole area) Lenehan calls into Lynam's betting shop (location unknown) to place his money on Sceptre. (The Gold Cup race, scheduled for three o'clock (GMT) had already been run by this stage, but bets were, apparently, still taken until the result was telegraphed through). Inside he meets Bantam Lyons about to back Throwaway on the strength of his 'tip' from Bloom, and (unfortunately for Lyons) talks him out of it. Lenehan and M'Coy walk on towards Merchants' Arch.

Detour: *Wandering Rocks xvi*

At Fownes Street turn right towards Dame Street, passing on the right Cecilia Street where James Joyce briefly studied in the Royal University Medical School. The building is now named Cecilia House. Directly opposite the top of Fownes Street at 33 Dame Street is the site of the DBC restaurant, with its present façade dating from the late 1980s.

> As they trod across the thick carpet Buck Mulligan whispered behind his Panama to Haines:
> —Parnell's brother. There in the corner.

204 Mulligan, having parted from Stephen on the way from the library, meets Haines, who has bought Douglas Hyde's *Lovesongs of Connacht* in Gill's bookshop in O'Connell Street (passed by the funeral cortège earlier in the morning).

'—We call it D.B.C. because they have damn bad cakes,' explains Mulligan. The letters actually stood for Dublin Bread Company, later Dublin Bakery Company. There were several of these DBC tearooms around the city; it was in this one that Boylan was introduced to Molly Bloom (who afterwards left her gloves in the ladies' lavatory). The window where they sat was a wide one, with a good view over the street. At the next table is John Howard Parnell, the city marshal and brother of the dead nationalist leader. Bloom saw him earlier opposite Trinity College, presumably on his way to the DBC. His unnamed opponent at the chessboard could well have been Joyce's friend J. F. Byrne ('Cranly'), who played chess here regularly with Parnell and devoted a section of his memoirs, *Silent*

Years, to accounts of their matches. Byrne's college nickname was 'The White Bishop'.

205   Over scones and butter and cakes and *mélanges* (coffee with whipped cream) they discuss Stephen Dedalus and decide that he is a lost cause. A few minutes later (page 208) they watch the viceregal equipage going past. (The interpolations in this section feature the onelegged sailor, who has reached Nelson Street, and the crumpled piece of paper thrown into the river by Bloom on page 125, floating 'beyond new Wapping street past Benson's ferry', practically as far as the present East Link toll bridge.)

Return down Fownes Street to Temple Bar and Lenehan and M'Coy.

Wandering Rocks ix (continued)

'They went up the steps and under Merchants' arch. A darkbacked figure scanned books on the hawker's cart.' Merchants' Arch gives access leftwards from Temple Bar to the river, directly beside the Halfpenny Bridge. This picturesque little thoroughfare is still lined with pocket-sized shops, and it is outside one of these that Lenehan and M'Coy spot Bloom (see *Wandering Rocks x* below). While Lenehan tells the story of the Glencree Reformatory dinner they go through the arch, across to the riverwall and left along the river. Bloom will follow in their tracks (see Tour 5a below).

(Interpolations in *Wandering Rocks ix* describe Richie Goulding outside the Four Courts, the viceregal cavalcade emerging from the Lodge gates,

Master Patrick Dignam leaving Mangan's in Wicklow Street, and Molly Bloom replacing the fallen card in 7 Eccles Street.)

Wandering Rocks x

193   Mr Bloom turned over idly pages of *The Awful Disclosures of Maria Monk*, then of Aristotle's *Masterpiece*.

Bloom, who left the library at the same time as Stephen, has travelled in the same direction – to the bookshops on the quays. Evidence suggests that he has already visited Clohissey's in Bedford Row, where Stephen browses a few minutes later. According to Hart and Knuth, Bloom is probably at Francis Fitzgerald's shop (now The Merchant Barber) on 194   the corner of Merchants' Arch and Temple Bar. He selects for Molly a book named *Sweets of Sin* (which the scholars have yet to identify, although a 'reconstructed' version was serialised in the *James Joyce Quarterly*) and rents it from the shopman, who appears from behind a dingy curtain strung across the back of the shop. '—*Sweets of Sin*, he said, tapping on it. That's a good one.' (Interpolations in this section refer to Denis J. Maginni, who has made his elegant way all along O'Connell Street to the Bridge, and to the 'elderly female' leaving the Four Courts.)

To follow Bloom on his way to the Ormond Hotel, see Tour 5a below. Otherwise continue along Temple Bar and Fleet Street to the junction with Bedford Row.

Wandering Rocks xiii

198   Stephen Dedalus watched through the webbed window the lapidary's fingers prove a timedulled chain.

Stephen, having left Buck Mulligan near the library and Almidano Artifoni outside Trinity College, is now outside Russell's the jewellers at 57 Fleet Street. The discomfort which he feels would doubtless be increased by the discovery that the premises next door is now a popular pub named The Oliver St John Gogarty. Around the corner beside the pub (which has no actual connection with the man after whom it is named) is a statue group portraying the young 199 Joyce and Gogarty. He hears 'the whirr of flapping leathern bands and hum of dynamos from the powerhouse' to his left, which has since relinquished its rôle to become a motorbike theme restaurant named The Thunder Road Café. Oppressed by the 'two roaring worlds' of time and space, he feels the urge to shatter them (as he does eventually, in Nighttown) but decides 'Not yet awhile.'

He turns and goes down Bedford Row. Clohissey's bookshop at Nos. 10-11 on the right has gone now, replaced by a garage entrance with large steel shutters. As he pores over an interesting book of 'Charms and invocations', he is interrupted 200 by his sister Dilly, who has crossed the river from Dillon's auctionroom and has just bought a French primer with one of the precious pennies she coaxed out of her father. (It is of interest to note that a French-English dictionary bearing the name 'John Stanislaus Joyce' and the address '7 St Peter's Terrace, Cabra' is in the collection at the Joyce Tower.) Stephen gives his approval, and inwardly stifles the urge to help his family, knowing that he will only sink with them.

This is the last we see of Stephen for some time. From here he goes to spend his money on drink in the Moira Hotel in Trinity Street and Larchet's in College Green, five minutes' walk from Bedford Row. (The interpolations in this section describe the two women whom Stephen saw on Sandymount Strand, returning from their expedition with their cockles, and Father Conmee, now walking through Donnycarney.)

Follow Bedford Row down to the river and turn right along Aston Quay, then cross the river by O'Connell Bridge and turn left along Bachelor's Walk, passing the entrance to Williams's Row.

Wandering Rocks xi

195   The lacquey by the door of Dillon's auctionrooms shook his handbell twice again and viewed himself in the chalked mirror of the cabinet.

The auctionrooms where Dilly has been loitering for the past couple of hours are now occupied by the entrance to the Arlington Hotel.

'Mr Dedalus, tugging a long moustache, came round from Williams's row.' Mr Dedalus has presumably come up Williams's Row from the Oval pub in Abbey Street, where he was drinking with Ned Lambert and other cronies. The lane has since been named Bachelors Way, but a rusted and almost illegible sign remains to proclaim the original title. Because the lane is obscured from this angle, Dilly cannot tell which direction he came from and thinks he may have been further away in the Scotch House on Burgh Quay. Bloom would also have come this way earlier from the newspaper office when he went to talk to Alexander Keyes here in Dillon's.

196   Dilly persuades her father to hand over a shilling and two pennies, and he walks on along the quays towards the Ormond Hotel, while she crosses the river to the bookshop in Bedford Row. (In the interpolations we see the runners in the College races, Mr Kernan in James's Street, and the viceregal cavalcade leaving the park.)

Continue with Mr Dedalus along the quays past the metal bridge, known as the Halfpenny Bridge because when it was first erected a toll of one halfpenny was levied on those who used it. Beside the bridge a restaurant occupies the former shop of the Dublin Woollen Company, for whom Joyce worked as an agent when he was in Trieste. Outside the Liffey Street front is a bronze sculpture by Jakki McKenna of two women shoppers sitting on a bench, jocularly known as 'The Hags with the Bags'. At the next corner on the quay is Swift's Row.

Wandering Rocks xiv

200   —Hello, Simon, Father Cowley said. How are things?
       —Hello, Bob, old man, Mr Dedalus answered, stopping.
       They clasped hands loudly outside Reddy and Daughter's.

Reddy's antique shop on Ormond Quay Lower was on the east side of Swift's Row, near where the Millennium Bridge for pedestrians now spans the river. Father Cowley (not a priest, despite his title) is
201 waiting for Ben Dollard, whom they see approaching from the metal bridge on his way from the Bodega in Dame Street. Ben Dollard is to intercede for Cowley with long John Fanning, the subsheriff, to call off the bailiffs placed on his house by Reuben J. Dodd. However it turns out that Cowley's landlord, the Reverend Hugh C. Love (who is not far away at that moment), has already distrained for rent and has the prior claim. Cowley's address, 29 Windsor Avenue, was a former residence of the Joyces in Fairview.

       They continue along the quay, past Grattan Bridge. Mr Dedalus visits the 'greenhouse' or public urinal on the riverside pavement just beyond the bridge, and the others go on to the subsheriff's office further along Ormond Quay Upper. The subsheriff is in fact across the river in Kavanagh's at this time. Shortly afterwards they all meet up again in the Ormond Hotel. (Interpolations here describe Cashel Boyle

O'Connor Fitzmaurice Tisdall Farrell, passing the Kildare Street Club on the corner with Nassau Street, and the Reverend Hugh C. Love passing Kennedy's at the corner of Mary's Abbey and Capel Street.)

Tour 5a: Alternative route to the Ormond Hotel
Sirens, 3.40 p.m.

Bloom, leaving Merchants' Arch with *Sweets of Sin* in his pocket, follows in the wake of Lenehan and M'Coy along Wellington Quay. As the action of *Sirens* begins in the Ormond Hotel, we get glimpses of him approaching in the distance.

212 'Bloowho went by by Moulang's pipes bearing in his breast the sweets of sin, by Wine's antiques, in memory bearing sweet sinful words, by Carroll's dusky battered plate, for Raoul.' Wine's at No. 35 is now Beads & Bling; Moulang's (now the Botticelli Italian restaurant) was at No. 31 (Hart and Knuth explain this inversion as typical of the musical techniques used throughout the episode), followed by Carroll's at No. 29 (now Locations).

213 'Bloowhose dark eye read Aaron Figatner's name. Why do I always think Figather?' He passes Figatner's the jewellers at No. 26 Wellington Quay and Prosper Loré the milliner at No. 22. The religious statues in Bassi's at No. 14 remind him of his unsuccessful attempts to inspect the goddesses in the National

214 Museum, interrupted by Buck Mulligan. He continues past Cantwell's at No. 12 and more religious goods at

Ceppi's (Nos. 8-9). In between at No. 11 was Roger Greene's the solicitor's office. Here, a few minutes earlier, Gerty MacDowell watched the viceroy passing by while Lenehan and M'Coy took leave of each other on the bridge. Bloom decides to eat before seeing Nannetti about the paragraph for Keyes; he considers the Clarence Hotel which he is passing (now an upmarket establishment owned by rock group U2) and the Dolphin in the next street, but goes on.

215   'Yes, Mr Bloom crossed bridge of Yessex. To Martha I must write. Buy paper. Daly's.' Bloom crosses Grattan (formerly Essex) Bridge. At this point, where the Poddle originally met the Liffey, was the entrance to the 'Dubh Linn' (Black Pool) which was situated behind Dublin Castle and which gave its name to the ninth-century Viking settlement that was formed on the river bank nearby at Wood Quay, location of the controversial modern Civic Offices which were built on top of the archaeological site.

216   In Daly's, the tobacconists on the corner of Capel Street and Ormond Quay Upper, Bloom buys 'Two sheets cream vellum paper one reserve two envelopes'
217   for his letter to Martha. Catching sight of Blazes Boylan passing in a jaunting car, he moves on an impulse to follow it and almost forgets to pay for the stationery. He tenders a sixpence and gets fourpence change.

       Boylan alights and enters the Ormond Hotel.
218   Bloom, hovering outside, sees Father Cowley outside Fanning's office and meets Richie Goulding approaching from the direction of the Four Courts. They decide to eat together and go into the hotel.

To find out what has been happening there in the meantime, we return to the beginning of the chapter. 'Bronze by gold heard the hoofirons, steelyringing.'

210   Joyce said that he wrote this episode in the musical form of a *fuga per canonem*. Its technique represents in words a number of musical devices, and the episode begins with a sort of overture which previews the
211   various themes of the piece. The action proper starts on the next page with the two barmaids looking 'over the crossblind of the Ormond bar' at the passing cavalcade.

The hotel has changed considerably since the first Bloomsday. In 1904, when it was run by Mrs Nora de Massey, the façade of the building was of a type with

20. Grattan Bridge. Daly's, where Bloom buys notepaper, is on the corner at the extreme right. The Ormond Hotel, with its entrance and windows painted white, is at 8 Ormond Quay Upper; the 'greenhouse' is outside it by the riverwall. Marks's shop is to the left of the hotel on the next corner. *Lawrence Collection I 2517, courtesy of the National Library of Ireland.*

the surrounding houses. Considerable alterations, however, were carried out after a fire in the 1930s, and successive changes took place over the years to 1998, when the name itself was changed to the Ormond Quay Hotel. For the past decade the hotel has been closed, awaiting the implementation of a plan to demolish and rebuild it. The entrance to the hotel is still in the same place, and the original bar was probably to its right with a window onto the street. On the left was the diningroom where Bloom and Goulding ate and where they could hear the music in the bar through the open door.

212   As the clatter of the viceregal hoofs dies away the boots comes into the bar with a 'tray of chattering china', and Miss Douce and Miss Kennedy drink their
213 tea despite a fit of the giggles over the 'old fogey' in Boyd's the druggist's. (Boyd's was at 46 Mary Street, next door to Dublin's first cinema, the Volta, which was opened in 1909 with James Joyce himself as manager. Joyce returned to Trieste within weeks of the opening and the cinema had to be sold soon afterwards.)

214   'Into their bar strolled Mr Dedalus. Chips, picking chips off one of his rocky thumbnails.' Mr Dedalus appears not to have accompanied the others to the subsheriff's office, having found the hotel too tempting a lure to pass by. He has barely sat down
215 with his whiskey and water and filled his pipe when Lenehan comes in, looking for Boylan. He left a message with Boylan's secretary earlier that he would see him here at four, his purpose apparently being to

interest him in Tom Rochford's invention. Lenehan
216 passes on greetings to Mr Dedalus from Stephen,
with whom he was drinking earlier in 'Mooney's *en
ville*' (Abbey Street) and 'Mooney's *sur mer*' (now the
Carlyle Club on Eden Quay).

(Lenehan's movements for the day are fairly well
documented. He first appears in the newspaper office
around 12.30, and then joins Stephen in the two
Mooneys'. Afterwards he calls in to Boylan's office
in D'Olier Street and then goes on up to Crampton
Court to meet Tom Rochford. The stroll along Temple
Bar with M'Coy fills in time before his rendezvous at
the Ormond. From here he will go to find out the
result of the race and then repair to Barney Kiernan's;
later he meets up with Stephen and joins the others in
Holles Street Hospital.)

Bald Pat the waiter comes into the bar to get a
drink for a customer in the diningroom. Mr Dedalus,
perhaps not too interested in hearing about his son,
wanders into the saloon, a separate room probably
situated at the back of the bar, and fingers the piano.
217 The instrument has just been retuned by the blind
stripling who left his tuningfork behind. Mr Dedalus
strikes 'its buzzing prongs'.

218   As he begins to play the piano, Blazes Boylan
arrives in the bar and orders a sloe gin for himself
and a glass of bitter for Lenehan. 'Wire in yet?' he
asks, referring to the result of the horserace. Both of
them have put their money on Sceptre.

219   Richie Goulding and Bloom arrive in the
diningroom and choose a table near the door. In

the bar, Lenehan persuades Miss Douce '*Sonnez la cloche*!' and she performs her party trick of twanging her garter: 'Smack. She set free sudden in rebound her nipped elastic garter smackwarm against her smackable a woman's warmhosed thigh.' This is another sound to add to the many musical noises in this episode – the cavalcade, the teacups, the piano, Boylan's creaking shoes and so on. The organ of the body which Joyce assigned to *Sirens* was the ear, and there is plenty to entertain it.

Boylan, aware that he is already late for his four o'clock meeting with Molly, tosses back his drink (a quick sloe gin, it would appear) and makes for the door before Lenehan can raise the business of Tom Rochford's invention. Lenehan gulps his bitter and 220 hurries after him. They leave the hotel and a minute later Boylan sets off in the jaunting car, along the quays, up O'Connell Street and North Frederick Street, along Dorset Street and into Eccles Street. The jingling of the car will soon be echoed in the brass quoits of Molly's bed.

As Lenehan disappears outside, Father Cowley and Ben Dollard come in from the subsheriff's office. They have, of course, missed Fanning, but Dollard assures Cowley that 'Alf Bergan will speak to the long fellow.' As they join Mr Dedalus in the saloon, Richie Goulding and Bloom order Power's whiskey and a bottle of cider from Pat, who gets them from the bar. Miss Douce is at the window, watching Boylan leave and wondering why her 'cloche' sent him going so quickly.

221   The trio in the saloon, unaware of Bloom's proximity, are recalling the night when Ben Dollard went to Holles Street to borrow a pair of trousers from Bloom for a concert. The trousers, as Bloom himself recalls soon afterwards, were a revealing tight fit. Bloom orders liver and mashed potatoes and Goulding has steak and

222 kidney pie. As they eat Ben Dollard launches into song: '—*When love absorbs my ardent soul…*' and Miss Kennedy serves two gentlemen at the bar. George Lidwell 'suave solicitor' enters the bar and is told that his friends (Mr

223 Dedalus and company) are inside. Rather than join them, he stays in the bar to have a Guinness and to flirt with Miss Douce. Lidwell was a real-life person whom Joyce engaged as his solicitor during the dispute over *Dubliners* with George Roberts, and with whom he had at least one meeting here in the Ormond Hotel bar; he was, however, ineffectual in the case and actually took Roberts' side.

     Dollard and Cowley try to persuade Mr Dedalus
224 to sing; but at first he only plays '—*All is lost now*' on
225 the piano, overheard by the diners. At length he sings, '—*When first I saw that form endearing*', and Bloom signals to Pat 'to set ajar the door of the bar' so that they can hear better. Listening, Bloom takes the elastic band off his packet of notepaper and winds it round

226 his fingers. The song, he realises, is from Flotow's *Martha*. '*Martha* it is. Coincidence. Just going to write. Lionel's song.'

227   Mr Dedalus finishes the song amid applause, and Tom Kernan turns up (we last saw him on page 207, vainly greeting the viceroy further along the quays at

228 Bloody Bridge). Half-listening to Richie Goulding, Bloom continues to fiddle with the elastic band until it snaps. He decides to write his letter to Martha here rather than in the post office, and asks Pat for a pen 229 and ink and a blotter. Pretending to be answering an advertisement, he produces his newspaper. 'He held unfurled his *Freeman*. Can't see now. Remember write Greek ees. Bloom dipped, Bloo mur: dear sir. Dear Henry wrote: dear Mady.'

Joyce himself used Greek E's when writing to a lady called Martha; this was Marthe Fleischmann, for whom he had a brief infatuation in Zurich in 1918–9. His letters to her, produced after his death, were at first believed to be fakes because of the unusual E's, but Richard Ellmann, Joyce's biographer, was able to verify them by reference to this passage.

Quickly calculating, he works out that he can enclose a postal order for two and six as a 'poor little 230 pres'. Finishing the letter, he murmurs, for Goulding's benefit, a false address while writing the real one. 'Messrs Callan, Coleman and Co, limited' come, of course, straight off the top of the Deaths column. He will buy the postal order at 'the postoffice lower down' on his way to Green Street where he has arranged to meet Martin Cunningham and the others for a lift to Dignam's house in Sandymount.

231 Through the bardoor he can see Lydia Douce holding to Lidwell's ear a shell which she brought back from her visit to the seaside. Bob Cowley is back at the piano, playing the minuet from *Don Giovanni*. 232 Appropriately enough, at that moment Boylan, of

whom we have been given periodic glimpses (as we were earlier of Bloom) during his journey through the city, arrives at 7 Eccles Street and raps on the doorknocker. No more is heard of him, but the rap is echoed by a 'Tap,' the sound of the blind stripling's cane, which is repeated over the next few pages as he returns towards the hotel to fetch his tuningfork.

Bloom prepares to leave and pays for his meal, but lingers when he hears Ben Dollard singing 'The Croppy Boy'. The story of the song comes through, bit by bit – how the croppy boy makes his confession to the priest and asks for his blessing before he goes out to die for Ireland, only to discover that the 'priest' is a yeoman captain in disguise. Bloom watches Miss Douce listening and thinks of the effect of music on people's thoughts and how absorbed she looks. He then notices Lidwell and wonders if the absorption is really for him. Certainly the motions of her hand on the beerpull seem to indicate something not merely musical in her mind.

Bloom takes his hat, abandons his newspaper and goes out past Pat, glances at the barmaids through the bardoor, and scares the 'eavesdropping boots' in the hallway. As he leaves the song ends and the trio return to the bar. Their conversation continues while Bloom, feeling lonely, turns right outside the door and walks off along Ormond Quay Upper. 'Wait. Postoffice near Reuben J's one and eightpence too. Get shut of it. Dodge round by Greek Street.'

The cider, and the burgundy from earlier in the day, are creating their own music as he walks past Barry's

at No. 12 (now a post office replacing the old one at
No. 34), and he is wondering how and where he can
238   exercise his wind instrument when he sees 'A frowsy
whore with black straw sailor hat askew' and recognises
her; he had once approached her in a lane but had been
scared off when she said that she had seen him with
Molly. To avoid her he turns and looks in the window
of Lionel Marks's shop on the corner of Arran Street
(now The Country Café). As the blind man arrives at
the Ormond Hotel Bloom views a print of Robert
Emmet in the window with the famous last words of
his speech in the dock: 'When my country takes her
place among the nations of the earth, then and not till
then let my epitaph be written. I have done.' The print is
possibly a souvenir from the previous year's celebration
of the centenary of Emmet's rebellion.

239   Taking the opportunity as a passing tram
drowns the noise, he lets his gases take their course.
'Pprrpffrrppffff.'

At this point one may follow Bloom's route from
here to Barney Kiernan's, or take Tour 5b below to
the location of *Wandering Rocks viii*.

Bloom passes Arran Street and goes on to the post
office at 34 Ormond Quay Upper, below Reuben J.
Dodd's office in the same building, which stood near the
corner of Charles Street and was demolished in 1998.
From here he apparently takes another circuitous route
towards Barney Kiernan's. He turns right either beside
number 35 or at the next corner beside the Four Courts.
(This imposing building by James Gandon, completed
1786–1802, housed the original four courts: Chancery,

King's Bench, Exchequer and Common Pleas. In 1922 its occupation by anti-Treaty forces precipitated the outbreak of the Irish Civil War. The building was shelled and countless irreplaceable archives in the adjoining Public Record Office were destroyed. The Courts were restored and reopened in 1931.)

At the back of the Four Courts he crosses Chancery Street (formerly Pill Lane) and is seen on the corner of Greek Street by the narrator of *Cyclops*, 'with his cod's eye counting up all the guts of the fish' (page 244). He appears to have filled in some time hanging round the back of the markets before heading for Barney Kiernan's, perhaps by going up Greek Street, turning right along Mary's Lane and taking the third turn to the left into Little Green Street. This street crosses Little Britain Street, where Barney Kiernan's pub stood near the opposite corner on the right. The action of *Cyclops* is described in Tour 8.

By returning along Little Green Street as far as Mary's Abbey, you may connect with Tour 5b, which begins back on Ormond Quay Upper.

Tour 5b: *Wandering Rocks viii*

From the site of Marks's shop walk up Arran Street and turn right into Mary's Abbey. On the left-hand side is Meetinghouse Lane, a narrow laneway in which is situated the old chapterhouse of St Mary's Abbey. Recently refurbished by the Office of Public Works, the chapterhouse now contains an exhibition on

21. The chapterhouse of St Mary's Abbey as it would have appeared in the reverend Hugh C. Love's photograph after the seedbags had been cleared out of the way. *Courtesy of Dúchas, The Heritage Service, Photographic Unit.*

the history of the Abbey. It is open to the public by arrangement (contact info@heritageireland.ie).

189   Two pink faces turned in the flare of the tiny torch.
—Who's that? Ned Lambert asked. Is that Crotty?

Ned Lambert, who has left the Oval pub after drinking with Mr Dedalus, is now showing a visitor around the chapterhouse, which is being used as a warehouse by his firm, Alexander and Co. J. J. O'Molloy, having failed to borrow any money from

Myles Crawford (page 121), probably joined the drinkers in Mooney's before going in search of his next touch, Ned Lambert. He enquires in the office on Mary's Abbey and is directed to the chapterhouse (page 185), where he finds Lambert with the Reverend Hugh C. Love, Bob Cowley's landlord. 'Crotty' is probably another of Alexander's men.

'—Yes, sir, Ned Lambert said heartily. We are standing in the historic council chamber of saint Mary's Abbey where silken Thomas proclaimed himself a rebel in 1534. This is the most historic spot in all Dublin.' All these details, and more, are available within. The room once lit only by Love's vesta now has the benefit of electricity. The chapterhouse, with its present floor seven feet above its ancient level, is all that remains of a flourishing Cistercian abbey, whose stones were used in 1678 to build Essex Bridge. The 'pillars' mentioned are probably a detail misremembered by Joyce. Love, who is writing a history of the Fitzgerald (or 'Geraldine') family, is interested in 'Silken' Thomas Fitzgerald, whose short-lived rebellion ended in his execution. A later scion of the family, Desmond Fitzgerald, a minister in the Irish Free State government in 1922, offered to propose Joyce for the Nobel prize for literature, but Joyce advised him against it, saying it would probably cost him his portfolio.

(In interpolations we see John Howard Parnell in the DBC and Lynch's girlfriend in Marino.)

190   Ned Lambert shows his visitor out, and follows with J. J. O'Molloy into Mary's Abbey. The clergyman turns left into Mary's Abbey and right into Capel Street

towards City Hall (page 201), but then apparently turns left along Great Strand Street towards Cahill's corner on Liffey Street Lower and Lotts, where he is understandably 'unperceived' when the viceroy passes. The other two go round to the courthouse in Green Street, where J. J. O'Molloy apparently does Lambert a favour in return for a loan. Like most other earned or borrowed money in this book, it is promptly spent on drink, in Barney Kiernan's.

To follow their route, turn right into Mary's Abbey and right again along Little Green Street, which leads to Little Britain Street and to the courthouse just beyond it on the left hand side (see Tour 8). Alternatively, turn left and follow Abbey Street to O'Connell Street for Tour 6.

Tour 6
Aeolus, Laestrygonians, Scylla and Charybdis, Wandering Rocks (vi, v, xviii)

Aeolus, 12 noon

96   Before Nelson's pillar trams slowed, shunted, changed trolley…

Halfway along O'Connell Street on the west side is the General Post Office with its imposing portico. Designed by Francis Johnston in 1815, shortly after the erection of Nelson's Pillar nearby, it was occupied in Easter 1916 by the Irish Volunteers and became their principal stronghold in the week-long rebellion which left most of the street in ruins. The GPO, gutted by fire, was later restored, and the site of the reading of the Proclamation of Independence by Patrick Pearse is marked inside the door. An extract from the Proclamation is displayed in the central window beside Oliver Sheppard's statue of the Irish hero Cuchulain, famous in literature for the unusual treatment given to it in Samuel Beckett's novel *Murphy* at the beginning of chapter four. At the time of writing, plans are in progress for a museum to be incorporated in the building.

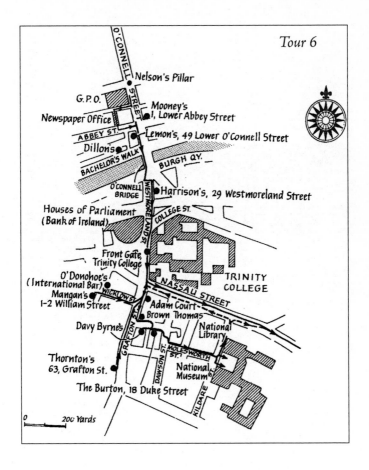

On the south side of the GPO is the cul-de-sac of Prince's Street. The area, now occupied by Penney's department store, was then the site of the ornate Metropole Hotel, on the corner with O'Connell Street, and the *Freeman's Journal* office behind it. Bloom's progress through the newspaper offices can be approximated by going into Penney's

22. O'Connell Street (formerly Sackville Street). Stephen and his companions cross the street past Sir John Gray's statue in the foreground. Before Nelson's Pillar trams, slow, shunt, change trolley and head in all directions. *Lawrence Collection NS 5383, courtesy of the National Library of Ireland.*

through the side door in Prince's Street and walking through to the exit in Abbey Street . 'Prince's stores' refers to the pub sandwiched between the Metropole and the *Freeman*.

Appropriate to its location, the episode is set like a newspaper in short sections under headlines. 'Aeolus' in the *Odyssey* was the controller of the winds, and Joyce chose the lungs as the organ of the body for the episode. Accordingly there are many references to wind and breath. People rush in and out, doors blow open and papers whirl about.

Bloom, who has returned to the city centre with the funeral carriages, is at the counter just inside the door of the *Freeman* office, where Red Murray cuts out a copy of the Alexander Keyes advertisement for him, and William Brayden, the owner, passes on the way to his office upstairs. Bloom takes the clipping through the building, 'along the warm dark stairs

97 and passage', into the *Evening Telegraph* office, which
98 backed onto the *Freeman*.

Here he sees Hynes getting his account of the funeral in to the evening edition. It is taken by the foreman, Councillor Nannetti. Nannetti, an Italian-Irishman, was indeed a councillor in real life and, as Bloom foresees, later became Lord Mayor of Dublin.

99 As Hynes passes, Bloom drops an unsuccessful hint about the three shillings which Hynes has owed him for the past three weeks. Bloom approaches Nannetti with the ad, which requires a change in
100 design, and offers to run round and pick up a copy of the redesigned ad that has already appeared in a Kilkenny paper. The foreman agrees to give Keyes a
101 three months' renewal, and Bloom walks on through
102 the caseroom towards the Abbey Street exit. Passing the *Telegraph* editor's office, he goes in to phone Keyes and finds Ned Lambert, Mr Dedalus and Professor MacHugh laughing over Dan Dawson's speech in the newspaper.

103 J. J. O'Molloy, a declining barrister, enters behind Bloom. He has come to see Myles Crawford, the
104 editor, in hope of borrowing some money. Ned Lambert continues to read the Dawson speech until

Mr Dedalus can take no more. '—O! Mr Dedalus cried, giving vent to a hopeless groan. Shite and onions! That'll do, Ned. Life is too short.'

Myles Crawford appears from the inner office, where he has been talking with Lenehan, the
105 correspondent for *Sport*. Ned Lambert and Mr Dedalus leave for a drink in the Oval pub (just outside the office in Abbey Street) and Bloom slips into
106 Crawford's office to phone Keyes as Lenehan joins the others. He is informed that Keyes is in Dillon's
107 auctionrooms in Bachelor's Walk, and goes out to see him (probably via Williams's Row, now Bachelors Way on the other side, which leads directly to the quays). The others, at the window, watch in amusement as the newsboys follow Bloom across the street, imitating him.

108   Mr O'Madden Burke, tall in copious grey
        of Donegal tweed, came in from the hallway.
        Stephen Dedalus, behind him, uncovered as
        he entered.

Stephen's companion is not to be confused with O. Madden, the rider of Sceptre, or Madden, the medical student in Holles Street Hospital. Stephen himself, who was last seen in Irishtown as the mourners went by, has stopped on his way here to send a telegram from College Green post
109 office. Now he delivers Mr Deasy's letter to Myles Crawford, who notices that a blank piece has been torn off the end. Stephen recalls to himself the lines which he wrote on the paper.

110   Lenehan, who seems determined to let the wind out of any conversation when it gets too serious, finally manages to parade his riddle: 'What opera

111 is like a railwayline? ... *The Rose of Castile.*' Myles Crawford, surveying the array of talents gathered in his office, encourages Stephen to write him something. 'Something with a bite in it. Put us all into it, damn its soul. Father, Son and Holy Ghost and Jakes M'Carthy.'

This was precisely the challenge which Joyce rose to in his own books, particularly *Ulysses*. The headline above this section, quoting Crawford's remark "YOU CAN DO IT!", has an unusual distinction in that it is the only occurrence in the entire book of conventional quotation marks, which Joyce normally never used, preferring italics or an opening dash. Presumably employed here to convey the form that a newspaper headline would have used, the marks only appeared for the first time in the Corrected Text.

112   Myles Crawford recalls a brilliant coup by the journalist Ignatius Gallaher (who appears in 'A Little Cloud' in *Dubliners*) when he reported on the Phoenix Park murders on 6 May 1882 (not 'eightyone' as remembered here), using an advertisement to provide map references. The victims of this famous crime were Lord Frederick Cavendish, the Under-Secretary for Ireland, and Thomas Burke, also of the viceregal staff. The attack was carried out by a nationalist group called The Invincibles, and, on the evidence of an informer named James Carey, Joe Brady and the other assassins were hanged. Fitzharris (known as 'Skin-the-Goat'), driver of the getaway vehicle,

got twenty years in prison and was let out in time to appear in *Ulysses*.

113   In the middle of Crawford's story, Bloom rings up from Dillon's to discuss the Keyes advertisement. The editor refuses to be interrupted and Professor MacHugh advises Bloom: 'Come across yourself.'

114   Meanwhile the conversation turns to the subject of
115   oratory. J. J. O'Molloy quotes a polished period from the lips of a fellow barrister, Seymour Bushe, and
116   Professor MacHugh answers with the lofty speech of John F. Taylor, which was delivered, not in the College
117   Historical Society in Trinity as stated, but in the Law Students' Debating Society of Ireland in the King's Inns in October 1901. Joyce selected this passage for the only recording he made from *Ulysses* – apparently because the acoustic recording was more suitable to a declamatory speech than to the quiet tones of interior monologue.

118   'I have money,' remembers Stephen, and he proposes that they adjourn for a drink. As they proceed towards the door, Myles Crawford goes back into the inner office for his keys, and J. J. O'Molloy follows him in, seeing his opportunity to ask for a loan.

119   The others emerge down the steps into Abbey Street and turn left. (The newspaper office was destroyed in 1916. The true location of the exit is just to the east of Penney's at No. 84, now a café, and not outside Eason's, where the pavement plaque was placed.) As the newsboys burst out behind them with the freshly printed racing special, Stephen starts telling his story 'The Parable of the Plums' about the two

Dublin women going up Nelson's Pillar. The tale is full of actions which are ultimately cancelled out by equal and negative ones. The money, for instance, is saved up, only to be spent; the plums are bought 'to take off the thirst of the brawn'; and when the ladies get to the top they get giddy looking down and a crick in their necks looking up, so they end up doing neither.

120   Myles Crawford appears on the steps just as Bloom returns from Dillon's. It seems likely that Joyce was misled by the confusing layout of the Thom's Directory listing when he placed Bloom as far along the street as the offices of the *Irish Catholic* (now occupied by the *Irish Independent*), as he would have approached from Williams's Row, practically opposite the *Telegraph*. Bloom breathlessly asks Myles Crawford if he will grant Keyes a free paragraph of editorial ('a little puff') in return for his renewal of the ad;

121   but Crawford uncooperatively replies '—He can kiss my royal Irish arse' and turns back to J. J. O'Molloy, whom he is also unable to oblige. (J. J. O'Molloy later gets money from Ned Lambert, but only in return for a favour.)

Leaving Bloom standing uncertainly in Abbey Street

122   (where we will return to him shortly), the pubgoers reach the corner, hearing the end of Stephen's story,

123   and cross O'Connell Street by way of 'sir John Gray's pavement island', where a statue commemorates the founder of the *Freeman's Journal* and inaugurator of the city waterworks. Here the professor peers aloft and to his left at Nelson on his Pillar, a doric column 134 feet high which was founded in 1808 to support a 13-foot

statue by Thomas Kirk of 'the onehandled adulterer'. Despite numerous proposals for its removal, the Pillar survived until the night of 7/8 March 1966, when the top half was expertly blown off by persons unknown. Army engineers blew up the rest (and shattered numerous shop windows) two days later. For a while afterwards, *two* heads of Nelson were on the market, but the real one is now on display in the reading room of the Dublin City Library and Archive. The Pillar stood at the intersection of O'Connell Street, Henry Street and Earl Street. Its site remained unoccupied until 2002, when it was replaced by a towering needle-like structure almost three times the height of the Pillar, designed by Ian Richie and referred to as 'The Spire' (various witty and scurrilous nicknames have been proposed, but none of them stuck). To this the statue by Marjorie Fitzgibbon of Joyce himself, nearby in North Earl Street, turns a Nelsonian blind eye. The statue of Anna Livia, Joyce's personification of the river Liffey, which reclined further up the street amid jets of water (and whatever was added to it) throughout the 1990s, has been moved to a quayside site opposite the Guinness brewery.

Stephen and the others are bound for Mooney's pub, which was on the north side of Lower Abbey Street next to the O'Connell Street corner. The pub exterior survives, but the Permanent Trustee Savings Bank now operates within. Nearby at No. 5 was The Ship pub, where Mulligan and Haines were waiting vainly for Stephen to make his 12.30 rendezvous. Between Abbey Street and the National Library

Stephen also visits 'Mooney's *sur mer*' on Eden Quay, travelling nearly on the same route as Bloom, to whom we shall now return.

Back outside the *Telegraph* office, Bloom turns right out of Middle Abbey Street and walks towards O'Connell Bridge.

Laestrygonians, 1.10 p.m.

124   Pineapple rock, lemon platt, butter scotch.
A sugarsticky girl shovelling scoopfuls of creams for a christian brother.

This chapter contains one of the most minutely detailed itineraries of the book and for that reason is especially rewarding to follow, so much so that in 1988 Bloom's lunchtime route was marked by a series of fourteen pavement plaques graced with the appropriate text. *Laestrygonians* begins outside Graham Lemon's sweetshop, where the incomplete remains of a sign reading 'The Confectioner's Hall' still exist above the modern shopfront. This stretch, between Abbey Street and the river, is the only complete block in O'Connell Street to have survived the destruction of 1916 and 1922; ironically, it has suffered more from an outbreak of garish shopfronts and fast-food restaurants which have sprung up over the past forty years.

Reading a throwaway which advertises the gospel meeting in Merrion Hall, he reaches the corner with Bachelor's Walk and glances to the right towards the

auctionrooms where he met Keyes earlier, noticing
that Dilly Dedalus is still outside.

125   'As he set foot on O'Connell bridge a puffball of
smoke plumed up from the parapet.' The brewery
barges, plying to and from the Guinness brewery,
had hinged funnels which were let down when they
passed under a low bridge, releasing the 'puffball'.
Bloom stops by the parapet, looks down at the gulls
and throws them the crumpled throwaway (which

23. O'Connell Bridge. Bloom buys Banbury cakes from the barrow in
the foreground. Ahead of him, on the extreme right of the picture, the
timeball on the Ballast Office shows that it is after one o'clock (and the
shadows confirm it). On the far side of Westmoreland Street is Harrison's,
to the left of the building with the two arched doorways. *Lawrence Collection
I 494, courtesy of the National Library of Ireland.*

is seen floating seawards in *Wandering Rocks*). From an applewoman's stall on the pavement he buys two Banbury cakes (made of pastry and currants) and throws them also to the birds.

126   Stifling an uneasy thought that Blazes Boylan might have a venereal infection, Bloom looks ahead to the Ballast Office on the corner in front of him. Now Ballast House, it was taken down in 1979 and rebuilt with some alterations, including the moving of its famous clock from the east to the north side. This was the clock which, in *Stephen Hero*, Stephen told Cranly 'was capable of an epiphany'. The timeball was part of a mechanism on the roof involving a copper sphere that fell down a pole at 1 p.m. precisely. Dunsink time (estimated from the observatory near Phoenix Park where Sir Robert Ball was the Astronomer Royal) was twenty-five minutes behind Greenwich time, and was official Irish time until 1914.

127   As he crosses Aston Quay to the Ballast Office the five 'sandwichmen' march towards him from Westmoreland Street, advertising Hely's in Dame Street where Bloom used to work. They spend the day walking up and down between the far end of Grafton Street and, probably, the far end of O'Connell Street.

'He crossed Westmoreland street when apostrophe S had plodded by. Rover cycleshop.' Crossing the street nowadays is a much more complicated business than in 1904. Bloom did not have to contend with cars, pedestrian lights, traffic islands and curbside railings on his way across to the cycleshop (the site is now part of a modern block).

24. Westmoreland Street. Bloom crosses under 'Tommy Moore's roguish finger' on the right, opposite the former parliament house on the left. *Lawrence Collection NS 5388, courtesy of the National Library of Ireland.*

128   Thinking of the old times when he was in Hely's, Bloom walks along the curbstone.

—O, Mr Bloom, how do you do?
—O, how do you do, Mrs Breen?

129   He meets Mrs Breen, an old friend, outside Harrison's Restaurant, now a newer establishment with an oriental menu. The pavement grating outside, where the street arab stood breathing the smell of the food he could not buy, has gone, but would have been approximately
130   where the plaque is now. Mrs Breen and her husband are on their way to John Henry Menton's office in Bachelor's Walk to take an action over an anonymous postcard reading 'U.p: up'. The most that scholars have

been able to make of this cryptic message is that Breen must have had some kind of urinary complaint. As Bloom learns that their friend Mrs Purefoy is in Holles Street hospital, 'A bony form strode along the curbstone from the river staring with a rapt gaze into the sunlight through a heavystringed glass.'

131 Cashel Boyle O'Connor Fitzmaurice Tisdall Farrell, also known as 'Endymion', was a well-known Dublin eccentric whose condition was reportedly due to a plunge into a vat in Guinness's Brewery (which was, in fact, full of carbon dioxide rather than stout). One of his tricks was to let off an alarm clock outside the Ballast Office when the timeball fell, which may explain his presence at this point. Farrell continues on his way towards the National Library, dodging outside all the lampposts. Parting from Mrs Breen, Bloom
132 follows Farrell past the *Irish Times* office at No. 31 and the crossing at Fleet Street.

'Luncheon interval. A sixpenny at Rowe's? Must look up that ad in the national library. An eightpenny in the Burton. Better. On my way.' (Rowe's would have involved a detour to George's Street.) Bloom passes Bolton's on the corner of Fleet Street and walks on towards College Street.

133 Before the huge high door of the Irish house of parliament a flock of pigeons flew. Their little frolic after meals. Who will we do it on? I pick the fellow in black.

The magnificent Houses of Parliament in College Green, designed in 1729 by Sir Edward Lovett Pearce and enlarged in 1785 by James Gandon, lost their occupation in 1800 when the Act of Union merged the Irish and British parliaments in Westminster, effectively ending the prosperous Georgian era in Ireland. The building now houses the Bank of Ireland, but the chamber of the House of Lords was preserved and may be seen on request.

Bloom passes the statue of the poet Thomas Moore with its 'roguish finger' and the nearby public toilet which gave rise to the joke about Moore's famous poem, 'The Meeting of the Waters'. At the time of writing, the statue has vacated its perch while work proceeds on the cross-city Luas line. In a less genial description in *A Portrait*, Joyce says of the statue 'sloth of the body and of the soul crept over it like unseen vermin', while Trinity College is a 'grey block…set heavily in the city's 134 ignorance like a dull stone set in a cumbrous ring'. For Bloom, the college has a 'surly front'. Founded in 1592 by Elizabeth I, Trinity has produced such distinguished graduates as Oliver Goldsmith and Edmund Burke (whose statues stand outside), Jonathan Swift, Oscar Wilde and Samuel Beckett. Its elegant buildings include the Old Library, containing its most famous treasure, the Book of Kells, an intricately illuminated manuscript of the Gospels dating from the ninth century.

Wandering Rocks vi

(188)   —*Ma!* Almidano Artifoni said.

He gazed over Stephen's shoulder at Goldsmith's knobby poll…

25. College Green. The tram in the foreground, with its conductor on the front platform, is travelling in the opposite direction to the one which Almidano Artifoni has just missed. Behind it is raised 'the stern stone hand of Grattan', and further back beyond the cab rank is King Billy's statue. *Lawrence Collection NS 5173, courtesy of the National Library of Ireland.*

Here at the front gate of Trinity, Stephen, on his way from the National Library to Bedford Row, meets Almidano Artifoni, the professor of singing. (The character is based on Joyce's teacher Benedetto Palmieri, and the name is taken from the director of the Berlitz School in Trieste.) Artifoni is, apparently, advising Stephen against abandoning his singing career. He had ideas like Stephen's when he was young, he says, he too thought the world was a beast. He feels that Stephen is sacrificing himself. A bloodless sacrifice, Stephen claims. Artifoni begs him to consider his advice, and Stephen promises to do so. Spotting the Dalkey tram, Artifoni takes hasty leave and trots in vain after it. He is obliged to walk to Ballsbridge, and arrives there just as the viceroy does. Opposite the gate, 'The stern stone hand of Grattan' is raised aloft on the (bronze) statue of the greatest member of the old Irish Parliament.

135   Bloom approaches the Provost's house on the left, built in 1760 and still lived in by the Provost of Trinity. A former incumbent of the office was Dean Salmon, whom Bloom remembers here. On the other side of the street he sees John Howard Parnell, the city marshal, with his 'Poached eyes on ghost', passing Walter Sexton's on his way towards the DBC in Dame Street for coffee and chess. George Russell, the poet (better known as A.E.) and a young woman pass Bloom on the curbstone; Russell, like Farrell, is on his way to the National Library, probably after a lunch in the vegetarian restaurant in College Green which he was known to frequent.

136   'He crossed at Nassau street corner and stood before the window of Yeates and Son, pricing the fieldglasses.' The opticians on the corner moved some years ago and the shopfront has been changed. Bloom looks up Grafton Street into the sun and holds up his hand to blot out the disk with his little

137   finger. He moves on past La Maison Claire, now a newsagent, and looks left into Adam Court, where he sees Bob Doran 'sloping into the Empire'. This is now Lillie's Bordello, the nightclub attached to the back of Judge Roy Bean's bar restaurant on Nassau Street. The establishment's most famous phase began in 1926, when Jammet's Restaurant moved here from

27 Andrew Street (where in 1900 Jammet's purchased Corless's restaurant, the meeting-place of Chandler and Gallaher in 'A Little Cloud' in *Dubliners*). Jammet's became a favourite meeting-place of writers and artists and its closure in 1967 was the end of an era.

'Grafton street gay with housed awnings lured his senses.' Grafton Street, still one of the city's most fashionable shopping areas, is now pedestrianised and has been repaved with stone slabs. Brown Thomas, the department store which Bloom passes on the left, moved across the street in the 1990s to take over the premises of its long-term rival

138

26. Grafton Street. Bloom approaches up the right hand side of this fashionable thoroughfare, passing the entrance to Adam Court beneath the clock. On the left are Switzer's and the corner of Wicklow Street. *Lawrence Collection R 702, courtesy of the National Library of Ireland.*

Switzer's. Their own site was sold to Marks and Spencer and still looks quite like it did a century ago. Passing here, Bloom considers buying a pincushion for Molly for her birthday on 8 September (also the birthday, as Joyce was mischievously aware, of the Blessed Virgin Mary).

Frank Budgen wrote of meeting Joyce one day in Zurich and asking after the progress of *Ulysses*. Joyce said he had been working hard all day and had completed two sentences. The time was consumed, not in choosing the words, but in seeking 'the perfect order of words in the sentence'. The lines in question, which occur as the hungry Bloom, caught by the sight of silk petticoats, daydreams of seduction, are: 'Perfume of embraces all him assailed. With hungered flesh obscurely, he mutely craved to adore'.

The corner premises, formerly Combridge's the stationers, are now part of the Marks and Spencer complex. Bloom turns left here into Duke Street.

On the left hand side of the street is the Bailey Restaurant, where Parnell and his supporters used to meet in the smoking room upstairs. In Bloom's time it was the haunt of Arthur Griffith and *his* nationalist followers, whom Gogarty later joined there. In the 1950s and 1960s it became a favourite meeting-place of Dublin writers, and for nearly thirty years it was the home of the front door of 7 Eccles Street, saved when the house was demolished, and officially unveiled by Patrick Kavanagh on Bloomsday 1967 with the words 'I hereby declare this door shut'. When the Bailey was rebuilt the door moved on to the James Joyce Centre, close to its original home.

Bloom's destination is the Burton Restaurant, beyond Duke Lane on the opposite side of the street at No. 18. 'His heart astir he pushed in the door of the Burton restaurant. Stink gripped his trembling breath: pungent meatjuice, slush of greens. See the animals 139 feed.' Repulsed, however, by the crowd of dirty eaters, 'He came out into clearer air and turned back towards Grafton street.'

140 Instead he enters Davy Byrne's 'moral pub', still flourishing at No. 21 but greatly altered inside. The nicely planed curving oak counter and the shelves full of tins are gone, and the walls are decorated with elegant murals by Cecil Salkeld, in one of which Davy Byrne himself appears in his later years, bald and with a large white moustache. Gorgonzola cheese sandwiches and burgundy are popular on Bloomsday.

As Bloom orders his burgundy he is hailed by Nosey Flynn in his nook. His gaze wanders over the potted meat on the shelves, reminding him of the Plumtree's ad placed under the obituaries and prompting thoughts of cannibals. The Laestrygonians in the *Odyssey* were cannibals, and appropriately for this lunchtime episode full of food and eating, the organ is the oesophagus.

141 He sits down with Flynn, who hears about the concert tour and asks, 'Isn't Blazes Boylan mixed up in it?' Involuntarily Bloom glances up at the 'bilious clock'. There are still two hours to go before Boylan's

meeting with Molly. (Joyce specified in his schema that this episode begins at about 1 p.m. If Bloom's observation 'Pub clock five minutes fast' is correct – and he checked his watch on entering the pub – he has taken at least three-quarters of an hour to walk from Abbey Street, a journey which should only take twenty minutes at most.)

142   Davy Byrne joins them from behind the bar on his way towards the window. Nosey Flynn is considering the runners in the Gold Cup, and appears already to have scanned the edition of *Sport* which emerged from the newspaper office on page 120 with Lenehan's tip

143 for Sceptre. Bloom briefly considers the dewdrop coming down Flynn's nose again, then returns to his lunch. About six o'clock, he thinks, Boylan will be gone and he can head for home. In the event he lingers out much later.

    He thinks of 'All the odd things people pick up

144 for food'. The sunshine and the taste on his palate bring back memories of the day in May 1888 when he proposed to Molly on Howth Head – the same scene which is in her mind at the end of the book. Studying 'the silent veining' of the oak bar, he thinks of the shapely curves of the classical statues in the museum. In contrast to humans 'stuffing food in one hole and out behind', the goddesses, he realises, are differently

145 shaped. 'They have no. Never looked. I'll look today. Keeper won't see. Bend down let something drop. See if she.'

    He rises and goes out to relieve himself in the yard at the back (probably where the exit to Creation

Arcade is now). In his absence Nosey Flynn tells Davy
146 Byrne that Bloom is a freemason. Although everybody
will admit that 'Bloom has his good points', nobody
appears to trust him entirely or to claim him as a close
friend. It is perhaps significant that no one he meets
is on first-name terms with him.

Paddy Leonard and Bantam Lyons enter, followed
by Tom Rochford. As they talk about the Gold Cup
race, Bantam Lyons claims to have a hot tip and
147 indicates Mr Bloom on his way out as the man that
gave it to him. After their drink Tom Rochford and
Nosey Flynn will go up to Crampton Court to show
Lenehan and M'Coy the invention, while Bantam
Lyons appears soon afterwards in the bookie's in
Temple Bar.

Mr Bloom meanwhile turns right towards Dawson
Street, avoiding the ravenous terrier choking up
its cud in Duke Lane. He passes the Burton and
William Miller the plumber's next door, considering
ways of watching the progress of material through
the digestive tract and calculating how much he will
earn if he can get Nannetti to insert Keyes's ad with
148 the accompanying paragraph as requested. He passes
Gray's at No. 13 (not, in fact, on the corner; Joyce
was misled by Thom's Directory which listed it as the
last number in Duke Street, the corner shop being in
Dawson Street) and turns right into Dawson Street,
passing Connellan's proselytising bookshop where the
Insomnia Café is now.

'A blind stripling stood tapping the curbstone
with his slender cane.' The street is clear save for

the Prescott's van outside Drago's on the near corner of Molesworth Street. The driver, Bloom presumes, is in John Long's (where Carluccio's is now), 'slaking his drouth'. He helps the blind man
149 across the street and follows him along the north side of Molesworth Street. The post office which he passes is gone now, but a pillar box of the period still stands outside.

The blind man turns left down Frederick Street towards the dancing academy at No. 35 on the right. Bloom, musing on whether it is possible to tell colour by touch, decides to experiment. 'Might be settling my braces' he thinks as he passes what is now the Jones Lang LaSalle office. 'Walking by Doran's publichouse he slid his hand between his waistcoat and trousers, and, pulling aside his shirt gently, felt a slack fold of his belly. But I know it's whitey yellow. Want to try in the dark to see.'

Ahead of him he sees Sir Frederick Falkiner entering the freemason's hall, on the left with its pillared
150 doorway. Passing a placard for the Mirus bazaar, he reaches Kildare Street and is just about to bear to the left towards the library when he sees Blazes Boylan approaching up the street. 'Straw hat in sunlight. Tan shoes. Turned up trousers. It is. It is. His heart quopped softly. To the right. Museum. Goddesses. He swerved to the right.' Anxious to avoid Boylan, he makes 'with long windy steps' for the gate of the National Museum.

This building, as Bloom recalls, built in 1890 to the design of Sir Thomas Deane, along with the matching library on the other side of the courtyard.

Before 1925, when Leinster House became the home of the Irish parliament, it was possible to walk straight across between the museum and the library.

To conceal his disquiet, Bloom pretends to be searching his pockets for something. The various contents of his pockets are unearthed – the Agendath Netaim leaflet, his handkerchief and newspaper, his potato good luck charm and finally the soap. Reaching the gate, he is 'Safe!'

Inside the entrance rotunda of the museum were the plaster casts of antique statues (since removed) which Bloom proceeds to examine, presumably using his subterfuge of dropping something behind the backside of Venus Kallipyge. Unfortunately, as we gather later, just before he can 'certify the presence or absence of posterior rectal orifice in the case of Hellenic female divinities' he is surprised by Buck Mulligan, who addresses a remark to him. After this expedition he crosses to the library.

Before following him it is worth visiting the museum, despite its lack of divinities. Its most impressive room is the Treasury, where some of the finest examples of Celtic art are on display, including the famous Ardagh and Derrynaflan chalices and the Tara Brooch.

Another curiosity nearby is Buswell's Bar on the corner, which, although it is not actually mentioned by Joyce, 'has been granted the James Joyce Pub Award for being an authentic Dublin pub' (according to the bronze plaque outside which quotes – inaccurately, alas – Bloom's thought, 'Good puzzle would be cross Dublin without passing a pub'). While Joyce would probably be surprised, given the degradations experienced by so many of his characters on licensed premises, to find the word 'Joycean' used in praise of any pub, it is true that the pubs in his works are generally places where the service is courteous and the conversation is lively and convivial.

Continue to the National Library by the gate from Kildare Street and enter by the door beneath the portico. Among the many documents of Joycean interest in the library's collection are some of particular importance. These include Joyce's fair copy manuscript of *A Portrait of the Artist as a Young Man* and the first copy of the numbered first edition of *Ulysses*, both given by him to his patron Harriet Weaver; a large collection of his business papers saved by his friend and secretary Paul Léon during the occupation of Paris and placed in the Library under seal until 1992; draft manuscripts of *Circe* and other episodes of *Ulysses*; early notebooks, and some of the earliest pages of drafts for *Finnegans Wake*.

The action of *Scylla and Charybdis* takes place upstairs in the Reading Room, which is accessible to those with a reader's card. At the head of the stairway leading up from the entrance rotunda is a monument to T. W. Lyster, the 'Quaker' librarian (who, as the 1901 census informs us, was in fact a member of the Episcopal Protestant Church of Ireland). To your right as you face the monument is the entrance to the reading room. Behind the counter inside the door is another door which leads to the office where *Scylla and Charybdis* is set.

Scylla and Charybdis, 2.15 p.m.

151   Urbane, to comfort them, the quaker
          librarian purred...

In the librarian's office are gathered William Lyster, Stephen Dedalus, John Eglinton and George Russell (A.E.). Stephen, who has had three whiskeys in two pubs since we saw him last in the newspaper office, has come to expound his theory on *Hamlet.* John Eglinton (a pen-name; his real name was W. K. Magee) was the editor of *Dana* magazine and a member of the library staff. It was he who met Joyce at the library on the morning after he left the Tower in September 1904. George Russell (who passed Bloom in Grafton Street on the way here) was a key figure in the Irish literary renaissance and a close associate of W. B. Yeats. As editor of the *Irish Homestead* (disrespectfully known as 'The Pigs' Paper'), he was the first to publish stories from *Dubliners.* His pseudonym was originally intended to be 'AEON' but a printer's error determined the name by which he was to become known.

The discussion which is in progress becomes a conflict between Stephen's Aristotelian logic and the Platonist approach of the others. Stephen's approach to Shakespeare to a certain extent reflects the approach which Joyce has presented to his own readers, that of seeing his writing as a 'portrait of the artist', filled with the experience of his own life.

Lyster is only destined to hear the conversation in part. Almost immediately he is summoned away

152   to the reading room by a 'noiseless attendant'. His assistant, Richard Best, 'tall, young, mild, light',
153   joins the group, having just seen off Haines, who has gone to Gill's bookshop in O'Connell Street. Best in later years was asked to give an interview on this chapter. 'After all, you *are* a character in *Ulysses*,' said the interviewer. Best retorted that he was no character but a real person.

154   Best raises the subject of *Hamlet*, and Stephen launches into his theme. He sails a difficult course, as Ulysses did in the *Odyssey* when he took his ship between Scylla, the monster on a rock, and Charybdis, the whirlpool. Almost inevitably he sees himself between 'the devil and the deep sea'. Carefully he sets his scene with a description of the Globe Theatre. 'Local colour. Work in all you know. Make them accomplices.'

155   Shakespeare, it is known, played the part of the Ghost in *Hamlet*. Stephen claims that he wrote the part for himself because he too had been betrayed by his wife with his brother. Russell feels that 'this prying into the family life of a great man' is unnecessary, 'interesting only to the parish clerk'. Joyce scholars would think otherwise. Stephen thinks of the pound he owes Russell, most of which he spent on a whore in Bella Cohen's (the same one whom he goes to see later, only to learn that
156   she is married). Because the molecules of his body have renewed themselves since he borrowed the money, 'I am other I now. Other I got pound'. On the other hand, his memory gives him continuity; he remains himself. 'A.E.I.O.U.', he concludes.

Stephen argues that Shakespeare's wife, Ann Hathaway, was of major importance to his work, though the others feel that she was merely a mistake. '—Bosh! Stephen said rudely. A man of genius makes no mistakes. His errors are volitional and are the portals of discovery.' This is a very useful remark with which to explain the occasional discrepancies which appear in *Ulysses*.

157   Lyster returns to the room as Stephen reminds his listeners that Ann Hathaway was older than Shakespeare and seduced him in a cornfield. 'And my turn? When?' he wonders secretly. Stephen, for all his self-confidence, is a lonely young man and longing for love. When he looks at the book of charms in Clohissey's later on, it is the one for winning a woman's love that interests him. He is ready for someone to come into his life as Nora Barnacle did into Joyce's at this time.

    Russell rises; he is 'due at the *Homestead*'. A meeting of the Theosophical Society may prevent him attending 158   George Moore's soirée later on. Stephen listens as the others talk about the evening and mention several of Dublin's prominent writers who are invited. His own name is conspicuously absent, though Mulligan has been asked to bring Haines. Moore is proposed as the man to write 'our national epic', a task which many would claim fell eventually to Joyce. Hart and Knuth have pointed out that Moore's soirées were usually held on Saturdays, not Thursdays.

159   A.E. leaves, taking with him a copy of Mr Deasy's letter for the *Homestead*, and the discussion is resumed. John Eglinton rightly points out that we know next to

160   nothing about Shakespeare's life. The books by George Brandes, Sidney Lee and Frank Harris which provide the sources for Stephen's argument are based very largely on supposition and very little on hard fact. Stephen is aware of the claim that Sir Francis Bacon was really the author of Shakespeare's plays and that 'cypherjugglers' like Ignatius Donnelly, author of *The Great Cryptogram*, had worked out that the printed texts of Shakespeare's works were in a cypher telling the real story of Bacon's identity (he was, it seems, a son of Elizabeth I by a secret marriage to Robert Dudley). However, he sails by this particular whirlpool and sticks to his theory. The period of Shakespeare's great tragedies indicates a time of sorrow and turmoil; 'the shadow lifts' at the time of the birth of his first grandchild, which revives in him his feeling for love.

161   Stephen claims that Shakespeare lost 'belief in himself' when he was 'overborne' by Ann Hathaway. Something in him was killed and he became, in a way, a ghost.

162   '—Amen! was responded from the doorway.' Buck Mulligan, the last person Stephen wants among his
163   audience, appears in the room. Best tells him that Haines just missed him and Mulligan explains that he came through the museum. Again the conversation veers off course into a discussion of Oscar Wilde's *The Portrait of Mr W. H.* which Best describes as 'the very essence of Wilde'. 'Tame essence of Wilde,' thinks Stephen, watching Best.

    'You're darned witty. Three drams of usquebaugh you drank with Dan Deasy's ducats'. It is worth noting that from this episode onwards we never see Stephen entirely sober. Others, however, were not so lucky. Mulligan produces the telegram which Stephen sent

164 him from College Green and describes the terrible scene in The Ship when Haines and he were waiting with '…our tongues out a yard long like the drouthy clerics do be fainting for a pussful'.

Having parodied Synge, he goes on to tell Stephen that the playwright is 'out in pampooties' for revenge after an insult to his front door (31 Crosthwaite Park, Dun Laoghaire, fifteen minutes' walk from the Tower). Stephen recalls Synge's 'harsh gargoyle face' from their meeting in Paris. Lyster is summoned again, this time to attend to Mr Bloom, whom he conducts to consult the *Kilkenny People* for Keyes's ad. As Harald Beck and John Simpson point out in *James Joyce Online Notes* (March 2013), Bloom is at another door to Eglinton's office, in a corridor beside the reading room entrance which leads to 'all the provincial papers' in the area behind the

165 librarians' offices. Buck Mulligan recognises Bloom and tells them what he saw him doing in the museum.

John Eglinton and Best invite Stephen to continue. Stephen explains that Shakespeare spent

166 twenty years living it up in London while Ann (left like Ulysses' Penelope) stayed in Stratford. We hear nothing of her in all that time save that 'she had to borrow forty shillings from her father's shepherd'.

167 Stephen claims that she had cause and occasion for adultery. If Shakespeare had not been wronged, he adds, why in his famous will did he leave her none of his possessions but his secondbest bed?

168   Stephen reinforces his idea that Shakespeare wrote from experience. A money-lender himself, he knew how Shylock operated. 'All events brought grist to his mill.' Current affairs and topical events provided the themes and material for his plays.

'I think you're getting on very nicely. Just mix up a mixture of theolologicophilological.' The theory, it seems, is more of a clever game than a serious belief. Diverted briefly by Eglinton's challenge to

169   prove Shakespeare a jew, Stephen steers back to Ann Hathaway, 'laid out in stark stiffness in that secondbest bed', and her return to religion in her old

170   age. Eglinton, however, still feels that 'Russell is right. What do we care for his wife or father?' Stephen, considering briefly the alienation between himself and his own father, describes a father as 'a necessary evil'. Shakespeare's father was dead when *Hamlet* was written; Shakespeare himself was a father, no longer

171   a son. His rôle in the play and in his life as playwright was that of a father and begetter.

Mulligan seizes on one of Stephen's remarks and has an idea. Lyster returns, and Stephen introduces Shakespeare's three brothers, of whom two, Edmund and Richard, are named in his plays, both in the rôle

172   of villain. Shakespeare uses his own name, Will or

173   William, here and there as well. '—You make good use of the name, John Eglinton allowed. Your own name is strange enough.'

Joyce chose the name 'Dedalus' for himself with care. In Greek mythology Dedalus was the 'fabulous artificer' who built the labyrinth in Crete and later made himself wings to escape from that country. The Dublin described in Joyce's books was his labyrinth, and he was destined to escape from it. Stephen, however, only has an abortive attempt to recall: 'Newhaven-Dieppe, steerage passenger. Paris and back.'

Lyster is called away again, this time for Father Dineen, the Irish scholar who is famous for his authoritative Irish-English dictionary, and Eglinton asks Stephen to continue his story of the brothers. Stephen thinks briefly of his own brother in the Apothecaries' Hall in Mary Street, on whom he sharpened his theories as he has since done on 'Cranly,

174 Mulligan: now these', and presses on, pointing out that '…the theme of the false or the usurping or the adulterous brother or all three in one is to Shakespeare, what the poor are not, always with him.'

He goes beyond this to claim that all Shakespeare's characters arise from different aspects of Shakespeare's mind. Their sins are his sins. 'His unremitting intellect is the hornmad Iago ceaselessly

175 willing that the moor in him shall suffer.' Shakespeare is a parable for all men, concludes Stephen.

Mulligan's idea comes to fruition and he begins to scribble on a slip of paper. Eglinton realises that Stephen's whole construction may be merely a *jeu d'esprit*.

—…You have brought us all this way to show us a French triangle. Do you believe your own theory?
—No, Stephen said promptly.

176 Eglinton feels that if this is the case Stephen need hardly expect *Dana* to pay him for the privilege of printing the theory. He is the only contributor who insists on payment. '—For a guinea, Stephen said, you can publish this interview.'

Mulligan draws him away from the Shakespeare fans (who remind Mulligan that he is invited to Moore's) with the hopeful suggestion 'Come, Kinch,

177 the bards must drink'. They leave the office by the door behind the counter and pass through the readers' room where Cashel Boyle O'Connor Fitzmaurice Tisdall Farrell is writing his name in the book. As they reach the turnstile at the door, Stephen thinks he sees a girl acquaintance in a 'blueribboned hat', but they pass on to the staircase with its 'curving balustrade' while Mulligan tells of the visit he and Haines made that morning to the Abbey Theatre. (By taking a train from Sandycove Station after their swim, they could have reached Tara Street or Amiens Street station soon after ten o'clock and stopped at the theatre on their way to The Ship in the same street. How long they spent in the pub is uncertain, but Haines must have left some time before Mulligan and visited Best in the library.) The Abbey Theatre was at that time still in the process of formation, with the movement of the Irish Literary Theatre society into new premises at the former Dublin Mechanics' Institute ('the plumbers' hall'), and the first opening night did not take place until 27 December 1904.

Stephen recalls a couple of points he should have made in his theory, but is swept on by Mulligan with his droll remarks and news about the literary people in the theatre. '—Longworth is awfully sick, he said, after what you wrote about that old hake Gregory.

178 [...] She gets you a job on the paper and then you go and slate her drivel to Jaysus.' It is small wonder that Stephen is not invited to Moore's.

In 'the pillared Moorish hall' Mulligan reveals the subject of his scribblings, a so-called 'play for the mummers', and laughingly reminds Stephen of a recent incident when he was discovered lying drunk in the corridor of the Literary Theatre's previous venue, the Camden Hall. This was based on a real incident. The 'daughter of Erin' who stumbled over Joyce's sprawled body was a Miss Esposito. When he was ejected by the Fay brothers, Joyce recovered somewhat and began beating on the door and shouting, 'Open up, Fay, we know you've got women in there.'

179 As they reach the exit door someone passes between them. It is Bloom, making his way like Ulysses between these two obstacles. Mulligan greets him a second time and notices that Bloom has taken an interest in Stephen, which he jokingly interprets as lust. They walk out under the portico and through the gate into Kildare Street.

From here all three travel in the direction of College Green, either by the same route by which Bloom approached the museum, or via Kildare Street and Nassau Street. Somewhere on the way Stephen shakes off Buck Mulligan, who goes to meet Haines in the DBC while Stephen encounters

Almidano Artifoni outside Trinity. Bloom heads for the bookshops off Temple Bar, followed a few minutes later by Stephen.

Turn right from the library gate and follow Kildare Street to Nassau Street. On the right-hand corner is the former Kildare Street Club, now the office of the Alliance Française. The magnificent interior of this gentlemen's club (designed by Woodward and Deane, 1861) has, alas, been removed but the witty carvings by C. W. Harrison (often attributed to the O'Shea brothers) may be seen on the exterior.

Here you may turn right to join Tour 4 at Finn's Hotel, or left towards the Grafton Street area to trace the routes of two Wandering Rocks.

Tour 6a: *Wandering Rocks v*

187   The blond girl in Thornton's bedded the wicker basket with rustling fibre.

Blazes Boylan, whom Bloom saw in Kildare Street about an hour previously, is now in Grafton Street at Thornton's fruit and flower shop beside Tangier Lane (now Dunne's Stores), buying pears and peaches for Molly. At the bottom of the basket go the port and potted meat, which he has presumably bought elsewhere. Outside the shop the Hely's men plod 'towards their goal' at the corner of Stephen's Green, where on page 188 they turn round and retrace their steps behind the intended site for Wolfe Tone's statue. (A foundation stone was laid during the Tone centenary celebrations in 1898 for a statue by John Henry Foley similar to his O'Connell monument, but subscriptions failed to meet the target and the project was eventually abandoned. A more modern statue of Tone has since been erected on a different corner of the Green).

'—Can you send them by tram? Now?' he asks, while in an interpolation we see Bloom in Merchants' Arch. A messenger boy on a tram from the corner of Nassau Street would reach Dorset Street and Eccles Street in about ten minutes. Boylan tells the girl 'it's for an invalid' and asks to use the telephone. His call (on page 189) is to his secretary Miss Dunne, who informs him of his appointment with Lenehan in the Ormond. Boylan then walks along Grafton Street towards Trinity College. Outside La Maison Claire he meets Bob Doran coming out of the Empire (page 202) and is seen by Master Dignam (page 206). When the viceregal cavalcade passes on page 208 Boylan is outside the Provost's house. Soon afterwards – possibly near O'Connell Bridge – he takes a hackney car (number 324, driver Barton James) along the south quays and over Essex Bridge to the Ormond Hotel (Tour 5).

Tour 6b: *Wandering Rocks xviii*

206   Opposite Ruggy O'Donohoe's Master Patrick Aloysius Dignam, pawing the pound and a half of Mangan's, late Fehrenbach's, porksteaks he had been sent for, went along warm Wicklow street dawdling.

Master Dignam, who came out of Mangan's (now the Meet & Meat café and delicatessen) on the corner of Exchequer Street and South William Street on page 192, is dawdling along the south side of Wicklow Street, opposite the International Bar, still with its fine interior and O'Donohoe's initials in mosaic on the doorstep. At No. 33, Madame Doyle's (now the Rockport shoeshop), he looks in at the poster for the Keogh-Bennett boxing match. On the opposite side of the street is the doorway of No. 15a Wicklow Street, where according to Bidwell and Heffer[4] the action of the *Dubliners* story 'Ivy Day in the Committee Room' is set in an upstairs room. Nearby, the Base Bar opposite Brown Thomas stands on the site of the Wicklow Hotel, where young Stephen in *A Portrait* heard the sound *suck* in the washroom.

In Grafton Street he sees Blazes Boylan, with a flower in his mouth, listening to Bob Doran outside La Maison Claire. Reaching the tramline at Nassau Street, he sees 'No Sandymount tram' and follows Artifoni's example by walking along Nassau Street in the wake of Artifoni himself, Farrell, and the blind stripling. Farrell, returning on his tracks, passes Master Dignam but the fact is not recorded. Finally, the viceroy passes him in Merrion Square as he stands waiting to see the parade go by. His route home, by foot or tram, brings him via Haddington Road (Tour 2).

Tour 7
Wandering Rocks xix –
The Viceregal Cavalcade

207   William Humble, earl of Dudley, and lady Dudley, accompanied by lieutenantcolonel Heseltine, drove out after luncheon from the viceregal lodge.

As with *Hades*, this long route is best followed by bicycle, or by car with occasional detours.

The viceregal lodge in Phoenix Park, where this tour begins, was originally built in 1751–4 to the design of Nathaniel Clements. Now known as Áras an Uachtaráin, it is the residence of the President of Ireland and is occasionally open to the public. Some minor roads in Phoenix Park have been closed and it is best to take up the route at the Phoenix monument halfway along the main road.

The park itself is the largest city park in Europe and one of the most beautiful. It derives its name from a spring of clear water (Irish *Fionn Uisce*) rising near the entrance to the present Zoological Gardens. Acquired by the government in 1618, the grounds were first enclosed in 1660. The monument was erected in 1747 by the then Viceroy, Lord Chesterfield, who also laid out the grounds.

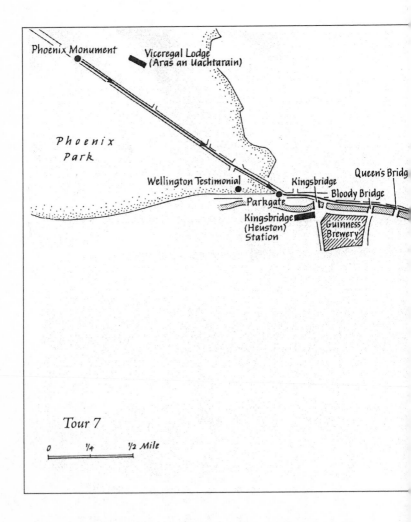

Phoenix Monument

Viceregal Lodge
(Aras an Uachtarain)

Phoenix
Park

Wellington Testimonial

Kingsbridge

Queen's Bridg

Bloody Bridge

Parkgate

Kingsbridge
(Heuston)
Station

Guinness
Brewery

Tour 7

0   ¼   ½ Mile

Drive from the monument towards Dublin. On the right-hand side of the road, just before the next junction and opposite the Viceregal Lodge, is the site of the Phoenix Park murders, now marked by a small cross cut in the grass verge. Also on the right, shortly

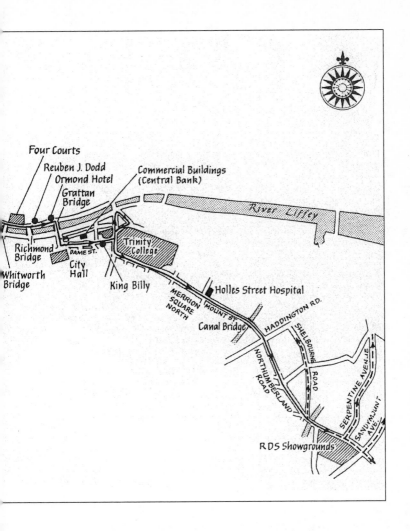

before Parkgate, is the Wellington Testimonial, a 205-foot obelisk designed in 1817 by Sir William Smirke. This monument is prominent in *Finnegans Wake*, as are the Magazine Fort, also in this part of the park, and the Mullingar House Inn in Chapelizod, south of the park.

27. Parkgate. 'Saluted by obsequious policemen', the viceregal cavalcade sets off across the city. To the left stands the Wellington Testimonial. *Lawrence Collection R 672, courtesy of the National Library of Ireland.*

'The cavalcade passed out by the lower gate of Phoenix park saluted by obsequious policemen and proceeded past Kingsbridge along the northern quays.' The gates at the Parkgate entrance were removed, together with their piers, for the Eucharistic Congress in 1932. Two of the piers were re-erected more recently as part of a plan to restrict traffic through the Park.

The cavalcade follows Parkgate Street past Kingsbridge (leading to Heuston Station, formerly Kingsbridge Station, on the other side of the river) and proceeds along the northern quays. On the left is the Royal Barracks, subsequently Collins Barracks and now the Decorative Arts and History section of the National

28. The Four Courts. The viceroy surprises Richie Goulding here on his journey along the north quays. Note the brewery barges on the river. *Lawrence Collection R 1655, courtesy of the National Library of Ireland.*

Museum of Ireland. On the opposite side of the river is the Guinness Brewery, followed by 'Bloody Bridge', a metal bridge erected in 1863 (see Tour 8). At the far side of the bridge is Tom Kernan, saluting 'vainly from afar'. Next comes Queen's Bridge. At the next corner on the left, outside the pawnshop at 32 Arran Quay, they pass Dudley White. After Whitworth Bridge the viceroy reaches the Four Courts, where Richie Goulding, emerging on his way to the Ormond, 'saw him with surprise'. Reuben J. Dodd's office, near the corner of Charles Street just after Richmond Bridge (the next block but one to the Four Courts) was above the post office (now demolished) at 34 Ormond Quay Upper; King's

the printer's was on the west side of Charles Street at
No. 36. Opposite is Wood Quay, site of Dublin's oldest
Viking settlement, where the Dublin City Council offices
now stand in front of Christ Church Cathedral. (The
river Poddle, which 'hung out in fealty a tongue of liquid
sewage', in fact emerges about halfway along Wellington
Quay from an arched conduit in the river wall; it may be
seen from Grattan Bridge.)

The viceroy passes the admiring barmaids in the
Ormond, and Mr Dedalus on his way across the street
from the urinal on the quay. (Hart and Knuth suspect
that his hat is brought low to cover an open trouserfly.)
The reverend Hugh C. Love at Cahill's corner can
neither see nor be seen by the viceroy, who is watched
by Lenehan and M'Coy as the carriages turn right across
Grattan Bridge (also referred to in *Sirens* by its earlier
name of Essex Bridge). To the left on Wellington Quay,
beside Dollard House, is Gerty MacDowell, whose view
of the cavalcade is obscured by the vehicles stopped in
front of her. To the right, on the corner of Essex Quay,
may be seen Sunlight Chambers, formerly the offices of
a soap company, where a coloured frieze around the wall
displays the various stages in the manufacture and use
of soap. Straight ahead is City Hall, built in 1769 as the
Royal Exchange by Thomas Cooley.

208

> Beyond Lundy Foot's from the shaded door
> of Kavanagh's winerooms John Wyse Nolan
> smiled with unseen coldness towards the lord
> lieutenantgeneral and general governor of
> Ireland.

John Wyse Nolan is at the back door of what is now the Turk's Head Chop House in Essex Gate, on the right. Lundy Foot the tobacconist had the building on the neighbouring corner, and the initials 'L.F. & Co' can still be seen above the Czech Inn. The viceroy goes straight on here, but motorists should turn left here into Essex Street (see detour below). Anderson's the watchmaker's was at No. 30 on the right, and Henry and James the tailor's shop was on the left at the corner with Dame Street. Though closed some years ago, Read's the cutler's, Dublin's oldest shop, still stands on the left at No. 4.

Tom Rochford and Nosey Flynn, who have just come from Crampton Court nearby, are at the top of Parliament Street (site of Dame Gate in the old city walls) watching the viceroy approach. Here the cavalcade turns left (a privilege now reserved for buses and bicycles) and proceeds down Dame Street.

Detour for motorists: turn left from Parliament Street onto Essex Street, and take the first right turn up a narrow street beside the Dolphin. Turn left to rejoin the viceregal route on Dame Street. (If the lane is blocked by an inconsiderately parked car you will have to drive on as far as Fownes Street.)

The viceroy and his equipage pass the poster of Marie Kendall outside the theatre, and the DBC tearooms at 33 Dame Street on the right. Directly opposite the DBC is Fownes Street, where 'Dilly Dedalus, straining her sight upward from Chardenal's first French primer, saw sunshades spanned and wheelspokes spinning in the glare'.

Dilly has come by Temple Bar from her encounter with Stephen in Bedford Row. Stephen himself, who like Bloom does not appear on the viceroy's itinerary, is not far away, possibly even approaching up Anglesea Street on his way to the Moira Hotel in Trinity Street. This would make him, again like Bloom on Wellington Quay, visible to the viceroy but unmentioned.

Beside Fownes Street is the enormous Central Bank building, designed by Sam Stephenson and completed in 1978. This controversial building was already under construction when it was discovered that its height exceeded by thirty feet the limit laid down by the Corporation planning department, and it was obliged to live for several years without the copper roof which now covers the top of the building and the huge trusses from which the entire structure is suspended. The Bank is visible for a considerable distance over the Dame Street skyline.

Part of the Central Bank site was previously occupied by the handsome Commercial Buildings, in which was located the Bodega wine store where Ben Dollard had been with John Henry Menton (before walking down Crown Alley, through Merchants' Arch and across the metal bridge in *Wandering Rocks xiv*). Menton himself now stands 'filling the doorway of Commercial Buildings'. The façade of the building which faces onto the plaza is a replica of the Commercial Buildings front, at right angles to the original position. On the Dame Street front is a round stone plaque of a sailing vessel named *The Ouzel Galley*. The plaque, which was originally placed over the inside of the doorway where Menton stands, commemorated a ship which was posted missing at sea in 1695 and on which insurance was duly paid. Five years later it returned, having escaped, together with some considerable booty, from the hands of pirates. The Ouzel Galley Society, formed to settle the disposal of the treasure, remained until 1888 to settle other mercantile disputes, and from 1799 met here in the Commercial Buildings.

Next to the plaque, on the left at 11 College Green, was the site of Larchet's hotel and restaurant, where Stephen spent some of the afternoon and early evening drinking. Before this he was in Trinity Street (opposite, on the right) at the Moira Hotel beside Dame Lane, now rebuilt and occupied by Harvey's Coffee House.

The Financial Regulator's offices on the corner of Anglesea Street are on the site of the old Jury's Hotel, which was demolished in the mid-1970s. Its Victorian bar, complete with fittings, was transported in its entirety to Pelikanstrasse in Zurich and reopened in 1978 under the name of the 'James Joyce Pub' (the precursor of dozens of 'Irish' pubs by the same name around the world). The hotel is mentioned in *Ulysses*, one of about sixty licensed premises which share that distinction, but there is no indication that Joyce ever went in there.

The next block was formerly occupied by Daly's Club, of which the central section, designed in 1790 by Francis Johnston, survives. The Club was not only the most luxurious in Dublin but also reputed to be

29. Foster Place. In this picture, looking across College Green from beside the Bank of Ireland, may be seen King Billy on his horse. *Lawrence Collection R 969, courtesy of the National Library of Ireland.*

the most profligate. The rather more demure Kildare Street Club was founded as a polite alternative.

'Where the foreleg of King Billy's horse pawed the air Mrs Breen plucked her hastening husband back from under the hoofs of the outriders.' The Breens, who have failed to meet Menton in his office, are now on their way to Collis and Ward's at 31 Dame Street in search of a different solicitor. As we learn on page 246, Breen then meets Tom Rochford, who sends him to long John Fanning; and from the subsheriff's office he continues up to Green Street courthouse. The equestrian statue of William III referred to here stood in College Green between St Andrew's Street and Foster Place, near the site of the present statue of the poet Thomas Davis. The statue, which also features in a comic story in 'The Dead', was unveiled in 1701 and became the subject of repeated attacks. Frederick O'Dwyer notes in *Lost Dublin* that after a bomb explosion in 1836 which 'unseated' King Billy, 'Among the first on the scene was the Surgeon General, Sir Philip Crampton, summoned by a message that an important personage had fallen from his horse in front of the Bank of Ireland.' It was finally blown apart in 1929, and all that now survives are some pieces of the ornamental plinth by Grinling Gibbons, preserved in the Dublin Civic Museum collection. Opposite Trinity College the cavalcade turns right from Dame Street, a manoeuvre now forbidden to all vehicles.

Detour for motorists: continue left past the Bank of Ireland into Westmoreland Street (right-hand traffic lane) and double back along D'Olier Street (centre lane) to College Street (left-hand lane) and round past the front of Trinity College. Do not try this between the hours of 7 and 10 in the morning and 4 and 7 in the afternoon, when private vehicles have to discover for themselves the concept of Dublin as a labyrinth. It will be necessary to turn right from Dame Street up George's Street and Aungier Street, left along Cuffe Street, around St Stephen's Green and finally down Dawson Street to rejoin the viceroy on Nassau Street.

The procession passes the Hely's men outside Ponsonby's at 116 Grafton Street. On the left, opposite Pigott's at No. 112, Mr Denis J. Maginni, who attracted so much attention on O'Connell Bridge on page 194, is 'unobserved' by the viceroy. By the wall of the Provost's house on the corner of Nassau Street, Blazes Boylan 'offered to the three ladies the bold admiration of his eyes and the red flower between his lips'.

209 The cavalcade turns left along the railings of Trinity College, listening to the music played by the 'brazen highland laddies' in College Park, where the College races are under way. On the right, near the corner of Dawson Street, they pass Mr Solomons the optician in the Austro-Hungarian viceconsulate; on the left at the far end of the railings, Cashel Boyle O'Connor Fitzmaurice Tisdall Farrell, returning from Merrion Square, stares across the carriages along the street at Mr Solomons' far-off head, aided by his 'fierce eyeglass'.

The carriages drive straight on into Clare Street without passing the back gate of Trinity in Lincoln Place where Hornblower the porter touches 'his tallyho cap'. Up until the 1980s the Trinity porters all wore hard riding hats with peaks. In Merrion Square they pass Master Dignam on his way home to Sandymount. Outside Holles Street hospital they pass the blind stripling opposite Broadbent's fruit shop (2 Lower Mount Street). Across their path goes the man in the brown macintosh, eating dry bread; he is next seen nearby in Burke's pub at closing time, where we hear that he is known as 'Bartle the Bread'. From Mount Street they cross the canal bridge (a famous 'Joycean slip' – it is the Grand Canal, not the Royal Canal) and drive on across Haddington Road (at the next traffic lights), where 'two sanded women halted themselves, an umbrella and a bag in which eleven cockles rolled to view with wonder the lord mayor and lady mayoress without his golden chain'.

The two women have come up from Sandymount Strand most probably by way of Bath Street, Church Avenue, Londonbridge Road, Bath Avenue and Haddington Road. Their observation gained an unusual complexity on Bloomsday 1982 when, in the re-enactment of *Wandering Rocks*, the parts of Lord and Lady Dudley were taken by the then Lord Mayor of Dublin (complete with golden chain) and the Lady Mayoress (to whom, romantically enough, he had got married the previous weekend).

The route leads straight on along Northumberland Road and past Lansdowne Road on the left. The house admired by Queen Victoria has not been identified, but Hart and Knuth have located at 14 Lansdowne Road the house of Benedetto Palmieri, part-original of Almidano Artifoni, who gives the final salute with his 'sturdy trousers swallowed by a closing door'.

It may be noted that, despite the assurance on page 207 that 'the viceroy was most cordially greeted on his way through the metropolis', he is in fact met with almost total indifference. The few 'cordial' greetings he does get either fail to be communicated or are given by mistake.

The viceroy continues towards Ballsbridge. To the right of his route is the circular American Embassy building, designed in 1964. His final destination is the Royal Dublin Society showground between Anglesea

Road and Simmonscourt Road. The handsome buildings date from 1925, when the RDS moved its headquarters from Leinster House.

From the RDS you may drive on along the main road through Blackrock, Monkstown and Dun Laoghaire to Sandycove for Tour 1, or left down Serpentine Avenue to Tritonville Road to connect with Tour 2. Alternatively, you may leave Ballsbridge by Sandymount Avenue (passing W. B. Yeats's birthplace at No. 2 on the right) or by Shelbourne Road, where from March to August 1904 Joyce was living on the upper floor of No. 60, on the right (now marked with a plaque).

Tour 8
Wandering Rocks (xii), Cyclops

A convenient point from which to start this tour is Heuston Station, beside the Liffey at Kingsbridge. It may be reached by the DART shuttle bus No. 90, which circulates around the quays between here, Connolly Station and Tara Street Station, or by tram from Connolly Station via Abbey Street, Smithfield and Kingsbridge. Before launching on the Joycean itinerary, it is worth visiting some of the notable buildings in the area. Just on the far side of the river is the former Collins Barracks, originally built as the Royal Barracks and continuously occupied by the military for nearly three hundred years until its acquisition by the National Museum of Ireland for the display of its collections. A visit here is an expedition in itself, however, and best left to another day. Also near at hand is the Royal Hospital in Kilmainham, which is within five minutes walk of the station on Military Road (to the left just beyond the station). The hospital, founded in 1680 by James Butler, first duke of Ormonde, 'for the reception and entertainment of ancient, maimed and infirm officers and soldiers,' is

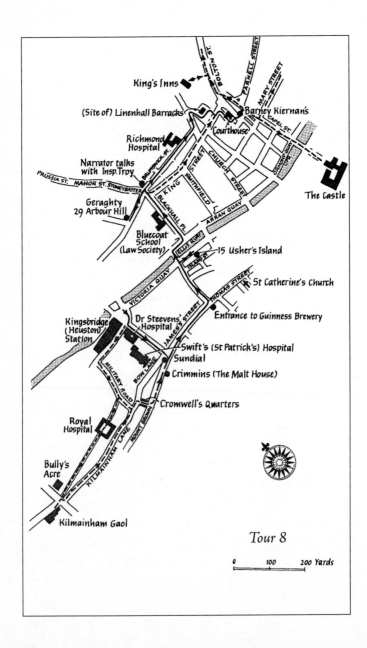

King's Inns

(Site of) Linenhall Barracks

Barney Kiernan's

Courthouse

Richmond Hospital

Narrator talks with Insp.Troy

PRUSSIA ST. MANOR ST. SIDNEYBATTER

The Castle

Geraghty 29 Arbour Hill

Bluecoat School (Law Society)

15 Usher's Island

St Catherine's Church

Kingsbridge (Heuston) Station

Dr Steevens' Hospital

Entrance to Guinness Brewery

Swift's (St Patrick's) Hospital

Sundial

Crimmins (The Malt House)

Cromwell's Quarters

Royal Hospital

Bully's Acre

Kilmainham Gaol

Tour 8

0   100   200 Yards

perhaps the oldest building in Dublin to retain its original structure. Restored and opened to the public in 1985, the former residential section is now the home of the Irish Museum of Modern Art, while the impressive Great Hall and Chapel are preserved for visits and functions. The Royal Hospital is open daily.

The avenue at the far side of the hospital building leads past an ancient graveyard known as Bully's Acre to a striking battlemented gate designed in 1812 by Francis Johnston, which originally stood on the quays at the foot of Watling Street but which was moved to its present location in 1846. Across the road on the far side of the gate is Kilmainham Gaol, built 1787–92 and finally closed in 1924. In its time it housed many celebrated inmates, including the Fenians in 1866, Parnell and his Land League associates in 1881, the Invincibles in 1883 and, in 1916, the Volunteers, several of whose leaders were shot here. With its classic prison interior, it has often been used as a film location. In the exhibition area, informative displays and memorabilia of the gaol's many political prisoners trace the history of the struggle for Irish freedom, while in a separate section the penal system in general is harrowingly explored through a series of interactive exhibits. Kilmainham Gaol is open daily.

Follow the outside wall of the Royal Hospital either from Military Road or from Kilmainham Lane to Bow Bridge. Here a set of steps named Cromwell's Quarters (known previous to 1876 as Murdering Lane) leads to Mount Brown. Turn left here towards James's Street.

Shorter route: Heuston Station to James's Street

If not visiting Kilmainham, follow Steevens's Lane from opposite the station (or take the tram to the next stop in James's Street), passing on the right Dr Steevens's hospital, built in 1720 by Thomas Burgh on a bequest from Dr Richard Steevens. Grissel Steevens, the doctor's sister, whose name appears with his above the east door, had rooms in the hospital and was reputed, according to legend, to have the face of a pig. The building, with its fine quadrangle, housed the oldest public hospital in Ireland until its closure in 1987. It now houses the offices of the Health Service Executive.

At the top of the lane on the right is St Patrick's Hospital, commonly known as Swift's Hospital after its founder, the celebrated author of *Gulliver's Travels*. Built by George Semple and opened in 1757, it is still a psychiatric hospital and contains some relics of Swift which may be viewed by arrangement.

Turn left into Bow Lane and immediately right into James's Street. Almost directly opposite, The Malt House at 27-28 James's Street was formerly Crimmins' pub, from which Tom Kernan has just emerged, glowing with gin and pleasure. A plaque on the pub commemorates its moment in literary history, and Crimmins' original nameboard can be seen displayed on the wall inside, to the left of the entrance. As this section begins Mr Kernan has just reached the junction of James's Street with Bow Lane.

30. James's Street. The rooftops in the foreground are those of the Guinness Brewery buildings on the south side of the street. Mr Kernan approaches from further along the street, near the church spire (which has since been truncated). Starting on the south side, he crosses soon after viewing himself in Kennedy's mirror, and walks along the sunny north side to the corner of Watling Street at the extreme right. *Courtesy of Peter Walsh.*

196   'From the sundial towards James's gate walked Mr Kernan, pleased with the order he had booked...' The sundial on its tall pillar, erected around 1813 by the Dublin Paving Board, was handsomely restored in 1995 and made the central feature of a small paved park with seats beneath its trees.

On Mr Kernan's right were Shackleton's offices at No. 35 (now a vacant space between the Oaklee Housing Trust and Steel Manufacturing Ltd). Mr Kernan is pleased with the way he has persuaded Crimmins (a tea, wine and spirit merchant) to take another order of tea – 'the cup that cheers but not inebriates' – from Pulbrook Robertson, for whom Kernan is an agent. His mind runs back over their conversation about the *General Slocum* disaster, an appalling incident, reported in the day's papers, involving a fire on a riverboat on New York's East River in which 1,021 people, out for the day on a Sunday School picnic, lost their lives.

197 Mr Kernan pauses to admire himself in 'the sloping mirror of Peter Kennedy, hairdresser' (a pharmacy now occupies the site). The frockcoat of which he is so proud did not attract the attention of Mr Bloom at the funeral that morning, although it is possible that he was not wearing it then. As he looks across the road at someone who looks like Ned Lambert's brother, he sees the only motor car to appear in the whole of *Ulysses*.

Walking on along the street, he looks ahead towards the site of Robert Emmet's execution, outside St Catherine's Church in Thomas Street. Emmet was twenty-five years old when he led a band of United Irishmen in an abortive rebellion in 1803. The facts of the uprising were familiar to Dubliners in 1904 after the centenary commemorations of the previous year, though Emmet's burial place is still to be established – Glasnevin, St Michan's, St Paul's and St Catherine's are among the candidates.

Opposite the top of Watling Street is the entrance to the famous Guinness Brewery, founded in 1769 by Arthur Guinness. Visitors, who no longer need to wait in the waiting room across the street, are now received in Crane Street (the next turn to the right), where the Guinness Storehouse is home to the visitor centre and a bar serving the celebrated brew.

198 Mr Kernan, however, turns left opposite the brewery (a Guinness-sponsored plaque on the corner records the event) and walks 'down the slope of Watling street', passing the Distillery stores on the right at the corner of Bonham Street. The distillery buildings, including the prominent but sailless windmill, are now part of the Guinness complex in the middle of what has been designated Dublin's 'Digital Hub', opened in 2003 as an international digital enterprise area. Mr Kernan passes Island Street and spies the viceregal cavalcade on the far side of the river, but is too late to register his greetings.

In interpolations in this section we see Bob Cowley and Mr Dedalus meeting on Ormond Quay, the crumpled throwaway floating past North Wall and Sir John Rogerson's Quay (which appear to move westward in relation to it), and Mr and Mrs Breen walking across O'Connell Bridge en route from Bachelor's Walk to Dame Street.

Just in front of Mr Kernan is Bloody Bridge, so named after the outcome of a riot raised in support of the ferrymen whom it put out of business in 1670. The original wooden bridge was replaced in 1704 by a stone one, which was in turn succeeded by the present metal structure in 1863 under the name of Victoria Bridge. Since 1939 it has been known as Rory O'More Bridge, after the leader of the 1641 rebellion who lived nearby.

Mr Kernan's eventual destination is the Ormond Hotel on the far side of the river, though what route he takes to arrive there on page 227 is not specified. He may have crossed here at the bridge and turned right along the north quays. Before following him, turn right along the south quays on Usher's Island. Here at No. 15 is the house where the Misses Morkan held their party in 'The Dead', the last story in *Dubliners*. The top storey of the building has been removed, but the first floor rooms, described in the story, still survive. John Huston's 1987 film of 'The Dead' used the exterior of the original building and accurate reconstructions of the interior. Left empty for some years, the house suffered at the hands of thieves and vandals, and is now in the hands of a new owner who has partly restored the building and arranged occasional reconstructions of the party and dinner described by Joyce. The front of the house looks directly onto the modern James Joyce Bridge, designed by Santiago Calatrava and opened in 2003. You may cross here to the north quays, or take Tom Kernan's probable route over Bloody Bridge and turn right. At Blackhall Place (directly opposite 15 Usher's Island), turn away from the river. On the left is the 'Bluecoat School', properly King's Hospital School, built by Thomas Ivory in 1773. Students in the school, which was founded by royal charter, wore the traditional blue uniforms up to 1923. When the school moved to new premises in Palmerstown the building was acquired by the Incorporated Law Society of Ireland.

Continue up to the top of Blackhall Place to the corner on the left where Arbour Hill meets Stoneybatter. Arbour Hill, as Joyce would have known when writing *Ulysses*, had become a place of particular veneration for Irish nationalism since 1916, when the executed leaders of the Easter Rising were buried here under quicklime at the corner of the barracks, at the far end of the lane. Wolfe Tone and the Sheares brothers were also imprisoned here at the barracks in 1798.

Cyclops, 5 p.m.

240   I was just passing the time of day with old Troy of the D.M.P. at the corner of Arbour hill there…

The anonymous narrator of this episode – known to scholars as the Nameless One – is a 'collector of bad and doubtful debts'. He has been trying to extract money from Michael Geraghty at 29 Arbour Hill (along the road on the corner with Chicken Lane, now Ardrigh Road), when, after an unrecorded conversation with a member of the Dublin Metropolitan Police, he meets Joe Hynes coming from the City Arms Hotel at 55 Prussia Street (a former residence of the Blooms, between Stoneybatter and the North Circular Road) where he has been reporting on the cattle traders' meeting.

As the narrator explains his business to Joe, we are treated to the first of a series of interruptions in

the narrative, written in a variety of 'specialist' styles according to their point of view. Thus the dispute
241 between Geraghty and Herzog is couched in legal jargon of the most pedantic character, while the description of St Michan's Parish is in the style of neo-Celtic romantic legend.

The pair walk to Barney Kiernan's 'by the Linenhall barracks and the back of the courthouse'. To go by the barracks they would most likely have gone along North Brunswick Street (but see the *Alternative route* below), passing the Richmond Hospital on their left. Founded in 1811, the hospital was rebuilt in its present Tudor style in 1900, and is now an education and event centre owned by the Irish Nurses and Midwives' Organisation.

All around them lies 'the land of holy Michan', the parish bounded by the North Circular Road, Dorset and Capel Streets and the river. It is named after St Michan's church in Church Street, with its fifteenth-century 'watchtower' and its famous vaults where bodies – some of them believed to be as much as eight hundred years old – lie preserved by the dry air, 'as in life they slept'. Among these 'warriors and princes' are the Sheares brothers, executed for their part in the 1798 rebellion, and Lord Leitrim, a particularly hated landlord who was
242 murdered in 1878. The 'shining palace' is the North City Market off Chancery Street, with its stalls of fruit and vegetables, while 'the herds innumerable' are flocking to the Cattle Market beside the City Arms Hotel in Prussia Street.

Beyond the Richmond Hospital and Carmichael House next door, North Brunswick Street meets Church Street, and originally continued on the other side where a block of Corporation flats now stands. Cross Church Street here, turn left up the hill and then right into Coleraine Street which leads behind the flats. Here, rejoin the original route by turning left into Lisburn Street. The Linenhall barracks, which stood to the north of Lisburn Street, were destroyed in the 1916 rebellion and have been replaced by housing. At the end of Lisburn Street turn right along Lurgan Street and left onto North King Street.

Alternative route via North King Street. The above route depends entirely on taking the phrase 'by the Linenhall barracks' to mean that the narrator and Joe actually passed the barrack building. On the other hand, the more direct route from Stoneybatter to Barney Kiernan's, along North King Street, still passes within a short distance of the barracks, and this is possibly what the narrator may have meant. To the right of North King Street is an extensive cobbled area called Smithfield, the ancient Haymarket of Dublin, traditionally known for horse trading and recently developed as a 'civic space'. A rival candidate for the 'watchtower' may now be the chimney of the old Bow Street distillery which has been opened as a viewing point.

Follow North King Street beyond Church Street and turn right down Halston Street, past the back of Green Street courthouse. This building was until 2010 the location of the Central Criminal Court and the scene of many famous Irish political trials, and in 1904 also housed the Recorder's Court. It is now used for civil cases. Robert Emmet's trial was held in the courthouse, and he and the Sheares brothers are commemorated by the monument erected in 1903 in the little park at the bottom of the street where once stood the infamous Newgate Gaol. The emotive inscription in Irish and English and the idealised figure of Erin with her wolfhound and cross reflect the character of Irish nationalism at the time. Cross the park into Green Street and cross again to the corner of Green Street and Little Britain Street. Just around the corner on the left at No. 9 is all that remains of Barney Kiernan's pub, which once also comprised Nos. 8 and 10. The present wooden front, dating from 2010, is a replica of the long-vanished original, of which a small fragment with lettering is preserved behind glass over the door.

In the pub they meet another nameless person merely referred to as 'the citizen', who is generally believed to be based on Michael Cusack, founder of the Gaelic Athletic Association. Joe buys three pints of Guinness with the money that he drew from the cashier in the *Freeman* before lunch, and the citizen accepts the drink while reviling the *Freeman*. He also pours scorn on the *Irish Independent* for its British orientation.

243
244
245

'As they quaffed their cup of joy', Alf Bergan comes in and hides behind the snug. Bob Doran is discovered 'snoring drunk' in the corner; it is not clear whether or not he has visited another pub in

the Liberties (the direction in which he was heading on page 202) before coming here. Alf points out through the door at Mr and Mrs Breen, who have come up from the subsheriff's office to the
246 courthouse, looking for libel action over the matter of the anonymous postcard. Alf, who works in Fanning's office, has apparently followed them up Capel Street to see the fun. He gets a 'pony' – a third of a pint of Guinness – from Terry the barman and hands over a penny in payment. Victorian pennies were, of course, common in change three years after her death, and were still in good circulation up to 1971 when old pennies became obsolete. A Joycean commentator, who shall remain appropriately nameless, misinterpreted the word 'testoon' as a coronation mug, involving Alf and Terry in a mysterious exchange of drinking vessels.

The citizen spots Bloom 'prowling up and down outside' and Alf produces some hangmen's letters.
247 Before the others can read them, however, alarm is caused by Alf's casual remark that he saw Paddy Dignam 'not five minutes ago' in Capel Street. Joe Hynes, who saw Dignam buried that morning, disillu-
248 sions Alf, and Bob Doran begins to weep drunkenly
249 about Dignam. A remark by the narrator clearly identifies him with Mr Doran of 'The Boarding House' in *Dubliners*, who married his landlady's daughter.

Bloom, who has been waiting around in Green Street to meet Martin Cunningham, comes warily in past the citizen's dog and is pressed by Joe to have a drink. In the end he accepts a cigar.

31. Barney Kiernan's. This is a late picture of Barney Kiernan's, where cases in the nearby Criminal Court were traditionally re-argued over a few pints. *Courtesy of the Dublin Civic Museum.*

The original of this episode in the *Odyssey* tells how Ulysses and his men were captured by the Cyclops, a one-eyed giant, and kept in his cave to be eaten one by one. Ulysses plied the giant with drink, telling him his name was 'Noman', and when the Cyclops fell asleep he blinded him with a burning stick. The other giants heard the Cyclops' cries but went away when they were told 'Noman has wounded me'. Ulysses and his men escaped from the cave and taunted the giant as they sailed away. Enraged, the Cyclops hurled a huge rock after them, which fortunately missed its target.

Various elements of the story are worked into this episode – nameless people, references to blind eyes and single eyes, treating with drink and so on. The citizen's 'tunnel vision' hatred of anything that is not

Irish is another form of monocularity. Bloom's cigar, of course, takes the place of Ulysses' flaming stick.

250 The hangmen's letters give rise to a conversation about capital punishment, which in turn gets the citizen
251 going on his favourite topic, great Irish nationalist
252 heroes and martyrs. Interpolated at this point is a melodramatic account of the execution of one such hero. F. L. Radford[5] has pointed out that the passage derives much from descriptions of Robert Emmet's execution, and that elements of this and some of the other interpolations in *Cyclops* can be traced to newspaper accounts of the following events in 1903: the centenary of Emmet's rising on 23 July; King Edward VII's visit to Ireland, 21 July to 1 August; the death of Pope Leo X on 20 July, his funeral and the election and coronation of his successor Pius X; and the huge demonstration on the centenary of Emmet's
253 execution, 20 September. Rumbold the executioner is named after one of Joyce's enemies, the British consul
254 in Zurich in 1917, and the hero's 'blushing bride elect' owes much to Emmet's girlfriend, Sarah Curran, who married an English officer of good family two years after the execution.

255 The citizen, Bloom and Joe get talking about the Irish language and the Gaelic League, and the citizen speaks to his dog in Irish, eliciting a few growls in
256 reply. Joe offers to buy another round of drinks,
257 which the citizen and the Nameless One readily accept; Bloom, however, declines, explaining that he is just waiting for Martin Cunningham to bring him to Dignam's house. That he has something else weighing

on his mind is indicated by his Freudian slip about 'the wife's admirers'.

258   Bob Doran passes on drunken condolences to Mrs Dignam and leaves the pub. With the new pints the others start talking about the foot-and-mouth
259 disease and the cattle traders' meeting. Bloom is dismayed to hear that Nannetti is off to London, as he had hoped to arrange with him the renewal
260 of Keyes's advertisement. Another matter dear to the citizen's heart, the revival of Gaelic games, is discussed. Bloom attempts to put a word in for more cosmopolitan sports like tennis but is drowned out by the citizen's rendering of 'A Nation Once Again'.
261 The name of Blazes Boylan crops up in connection with the boxing match which he organised; Bloom, painfully aware that Boylan is indulging in a particular form of athletics at that moment, tries unsuccessfully
262 to steer the conversation back to tennis. Inevitably the forthcoming concert tour is mentioned and the narrator notices Bloom's discomfort.

    J. J. O'Molloy and Ned Lambert enter the pub. J. J. has now got money, apparently from Ned, for
263 whom he buys a whiskey. In return for the loan he has done Ned a favour at the courthouse, probably, as the narrator suspects, 'getting him off the grand jury list'. They bring the others up to date on the Breen story, the latest news being that Corny Kelleher has advised Breen to have the handwriting on the postcard examined. Alf Bergan is accused of sending
264 the postcard, and does not altogether deny it. He appears to go rather quiet when J. J. O'Molloy, the

barrister, gives his opinion that Breen has got grounds for a libel action. 'Who wants your opinion?' thinks the narrator to himself, half expecting the lawyer to claim his 'six and eightpence' for advice. Just then the Breens pass the door again with Corny Kelleher.

265 The citizen begins to mutter about foreigners 'coming over here to Ireland filling the country with bugs', and Bloom, at whom the remark appears to be directed, pretends not to have heard. Instead he reminds Joe about the money still owed to him, 'telling him he needn't trouble about that little matter till the first but if he would just say a word to Mr Crawford'. Having lost Nannetti, he still hopes to get Myles Crawford's co-operation in the renewal of the ad.

266 The citizen, still trying to provoke Bloom, mentions the affair between Dermot MacMurrough and Dervorgilla which first brought 'the Saxon robbers' to Ireland. Alf and Terry are giggling over a modern-day adulteress in the *Police Gazette*.

'So anyhow in came John Wyse Nolan and Lenehan with him with a face on him as long as a late breakfast.' Nolan has been at the meeting about the Irish language in City Hall; Lenehan, who was last seen leaving the Ormond Hotel at four o'clock, has met him on the way somewhere, having also found out the result of

267 the Gold Cup race. Throwaway, the outsider, has come first and his own tip, Sceptre, is 'still running'. The citizen, meanwhile, is holding forth about Ireland's

268 great resources and her opportunities for trade, ruined by 'the yellowjohns of Anglia'. He looks forward to the day when Ireland will be a nation once again.

269   John Wyse Nolan orders a 'half one…and a hands up' for himself and Lenehan, which Terry correctly interprets as a 'small whisky and a bottle of Allsop'. It will have been noticed by now that none of the drinkers ever orders a drink by its proper name; this is typical of the innuendo and inferential language in

270   which the entire episode is written. Encouraged by the others, the citizen inveighs against the Royal Navy and the British Empire 'of drudges and whipped serfs'. Bloom's protest, 'isn't discipline the same everywhere?', is ignored as the others hurl abuse at

271   the British and their European neighbours. Joe buys a third pint for the narrator and the citizen, who show no sign of returning the favour.

        Bloom, goaded into losing his cool, tries to speak out against persecution and 'national hatred among

272   nations,' but gets laughed at. His claim to be Irish elicits an expressive spit from the citizen, and he lacks

273   the eloquence to make his point that life is about love instead of hatred. Suddenly he breaks off and leaves the pub to see if Martin Cunningham is at the courthouse.

274   The others settle back to their drinks and the citizen reads them a skit from the *United Irishman*. Then Lenehan leaps to a conclusion. '—Bloom, says he. The courthouse is a blind. He had a few bob on *Throwaway* and he's gone to gather in the shekels.'

275   The narrator goes out the back to consider this information while relieving himself. He has already consumed two of the three pints Joe has bought him, and another one cadged off an unnamed person

earlier in Slattery's (Suffolk House in Suffolk Street), and has a good load to let off.

Back inside, John Wyse Nolan is claiming that Bloom has been working behind the scenes with Arthur Griffith, leader of the Sinn Féin nationalist movement. Martin Cunningham arrives on the castle car with Jack Power and Crofton, an 'orangeman' or loyalist who appears in 276 'Ivy Day in the Committee Room' in *Dubliners*. Crofton, whose politics would normally put him in opposition to the citizen, sides with the others in denouncing Bloom. 277 Even the reasonable Martin Cunningham fails to defuse their hatred.

Ned Lambert buys drinks for the three new arrivals and Martin Cunningham's toast 'God bless all here' 278 prompts an interpolation describing an enormous procession of saints marching across the city to bless 279 the pub. The narrator, having almost finished his pint, is looking around in hopes of being offered another one when Bloom returns. Martin Cunningham, aware of the ugly mood in the pub, quickly gathers his party onto the 280 jaunting car outside the door. The citizen, with Joe and Alf trying to hold him back, staggers after them and shouts '—Three cheers for Israel!' attracting the attention of 'all the ragamuffins and sluts of the nation'. Bloom stands up on the car and boldly retorts '—Your God 281 was a jew. Christ was a jew like me.' The citizen grabs the empty biscuit-tin from the pub and hurls it after Bloom, but as his target is heading into the sun he is, like the Cyclops, blinded and causes no injury. An interpolation, 282 however, describes the impact as cataclysmic, leaving in ruins the courthouse and all surrounding buildings.

283   The car gathers speed and is last seen heading southwards down Little Green Street past Donohoe's pub (which was on the right opposite where Keeling's warehouse now stands) 'like a shot off a shovel'.

Bloom now travels to Sandymount, probably via Arran Street, the north quays, O'Connell Bridge and back along the funeral route to 9 Newbridge Avenue.

At the east end of Little Britain Street is Capel Street, where three alternatives present themselves.

A. Turn left and follow Capel Street into Bolton Street. On the left is Henrietta Street, leading to the King's Inns where Chandler works in 'A Little Cloud' in *Dubliners*. Bolton Street continues into Dorset Street, leading to Eccles Street (Tour 3).

B. Turn right along Capel Street and left along Mary Street. On the right is St Mary's Church, founded in 1627 and now a bar, nightclub and restaurant. Richard Brinsley Sheridan, Wolfe Tone and Seán O'Casey were among those baptised here. Nearly opposite at No. 45, now the east end of Penney's department store, is a plaque commemorating the Volta Cinema, which was opened in this building by James Joyce in 1909 and closed in 1948. Follow Mary Street and Henry Street to O'Connell Street for Tour 6.

C. Turn right and follow Capel Street to the quays near the Ormond Hotel, and across the river up Parliament Street and Cork Hill to Dublin Castle for Tour 5.

Notes

1. 'The Best Recent Scholarship in Joyce', *James Joyce Quarterly*, vol. 23, no. 3 (1986).

2. *Bloomsday: The Eleventh Hour – A Quest for the Vacant Place,* Carole Brown and Leo Knuth (A Wake Newslitter Press, 1981).
   'In the carriage for Paddy Dignam's funeral: Bloom was right all along', Harald Beck and John Simpson, *James Joyce Online Notes,* February 2014.

3. 'The Discovery of *Ruby*', Mary Power, *James Joyce Quarterly*, vol. 18, no. 2 (1981).

4. Bruce Bidwell and Linda Heffer: *The Joycean Way – A Topographic Guide to Dubliners and A Portrait of the Artist as a Young Man* (Wolfhound Press, 1981).

5. 'King, Pope and Hero-Martyr: *Ulysses* and the Nightmare of Irish History', *James Joyce Quarterly*, vol. 15, no. 4 (1978).

Appendix I
The Movements of Leopold Bloom and Stephen Dedalus on 16 June 1904

Leopold Bloom

8.00-8.45 a.m. *Calypso*:
7 Eccles Street and Dlugacz's.

8.45-9.45 a.m. Eccles Street to
Sir John Rogerson's Quay.

9.45-10.30 a.m. *Lotuseaters*:
Sir John Rogerson's Quay to
Lincoln Place.

10.30-11.00 a.m. Leinster Street
baths; Sandymount tram to
Haddington Road and
Newbridge Avenue.

11.00 a.m.-12.15 p.m. *Hades*:
Sandymount to Glasnevin. Coaches
return mourners to city centre.

Stephen Dedalus

8.00-8.45 a.m. *Telemachus*:
Joyce Tower and Forty Foot.

8.45-9.45 a.m. Joyce Tower to Mr
Deasy's school; lesson starting
9.00 a.m.

9.45-10.05 a.m. *Nestor*:
Mr Deasy's school, Summerfield,
Dalkey Avenue.

10.05-10.40 a.m. Dalkey to
Sandymount via Lansdowne
Road station.

10.40-11.10 a.m. *Proteus*:
Sandymount Strand. Ringsend to
Irishtown.

11.10 a.m.-12.15 p.m. Walks into
town along funeral route. Visits
College Green P.O.

Leopold Bloom	Stephen Dedalus
12.15-1.10 p.m. *Aeolus*: Newspaper office; visits Keyes in Bachelor's Walk and returns.	12.15-1.10 p.m. *Aeolus*: Newspaper office; across O'Connell Street to Mooney's in Abbey Street.
1.10-2.10 p.m. *Laestrygonians*: Abbey Street to Kildare Street via Davy Byrne's.	1.10-2.10 p.m. Drinking in Mooney's *en ville* (Abbey Street) and *sur mer* (Eden Quay); proceeds to National Library, probably by the same route as Bloom.
2.10-2.55 p.m. *Scylla and Charybdis*: National Museum, National Library.	2.10-2.55 p.m. *Scylla and Charybdis*: National Library.
2.55-3.40 p.m. *Wandering Rocks*: From National Library to Bedford Row, Merchants' Arch and Wellington Quay.	2.55-3.40 p.m. *Wandering Rocks*: Walks to the front gate of Trinity College and meets Almidano Artifoni. Continues to Fleet Street and Bedford Row.
3.40-4.30 p.m. *Sirens*: Wellington Quay to the Ormond Hotel, and thence to Marks's on Ormond Quay.	3.40 p.m. onwards. Spent some or all of the next six hours drinking in the Moira, 15 Trinity Street, and Larchet's, 11 College Green, eventually reaching Holles Street hospital with the medical students.
4.30-5.45 p.m. *Cyclops*: Via Chancery Street, Greek Street, Mary's Lane and Little Green Street to Barney Kiernan's in Little Britain Street.	

Leopold Bloom	*Stephen Dedalus*
5.45-6.00 p.m. By jaunting car from Barney Kiernan's via (probably) Little Green Street, Arran Street, north quays, O'Connell Bridge, D'Olier Street and Brunswick (Pearse) Street to 9 Newbridge Avenue.	
6.00-8.25 p.m. 9 Newbridge Avenue, and thence to Sandymount Strand via Leahy's Terrace.	
8.25-9.00 p.m. *Nausikaa*: Sandymount Strand.	
9.00-10.00 p.m. Sandymount Strand, and thence by tram to Holles Street Hospital.	
10.00-11.15 p.m. *Oxen of the Sun*: Holles Street Hospital, and thence to Burke's pub and via Denzille Lane to Westland Row.	10.00-11.15 p.m. *Oxen of the Sun*: Holles Street Hospital, Burke's pub to Westland Row.
11.15-11.35 p.m. Westland Row Station to Amiens Street Station.	11.15-11.25 p.m. Westland Row Station to Amiens Street Station.
11.35 p.m.-12.40 a.m. *Circe*: Amiens Street, Talbot Street, Mabbot Street, Bella Cohen's in Tyrone Street, and Beaver Street.	11.25 p.m.-12.40 a.m. *Circe*: Amiens Street to Bella Cohen's and Beaver Street.

Leopold Bloom

12.40-1.00 a.m. *Eumaeus:*
Beaver Street to Amiens Street,
Store Street and Butt Bridge.

1.00-2.00 a.m. *Ithaca*:
Butt Bridge to Gardiner Street,
Gardiner Place, North Temple
Street and 7 Eccles
Street.

2.00 a.m. onwards. *Penelope*:
Asleep in 7 Eccles Street.

Stephen Dedalus

12.40-1.00 a.m. *Eumaeus*:
Beaver Street to Amiens Street,
Store Street and Butt Bridge.

1.00-2.00 a.m. *Ithaca*:
Butt Bridge to 7 Eccles Street,
and thence into the unknown.

Appendix II
Ulysses: The Corrected Text

The text to which this guide refers is the 1986 edition of *Ulysses*, known as 'The Corrected Text', which laid down a standard text with identical lines and page numbers in all British and American editions, hardback and paperback.

The 'corrected' edition was made necessary by the fact that every single previous edition contained large quantities of typographical errors, omissions and unintended variations overlooked at the time of the original publication in 1922 and subsequently perpetuated. The task was not just a simple one of referring to the original manuscript of the novel, since Joyce made substantial revisions and additions on typescripts and several sets of proofs, amounting to approximately 25 per cent of the final text. The combination of an American publisher, a French printer and typesetter, and typists of various nationalities, all trying to interpret the difficult handwriting and unpredictable syntax of a half-blind Irish genius, was only part of the story.

The editors of the 1986 edition, in their search for an 'ideal' text, had to spend seven years collating and assessing every known variation on the text of *Ulysses* that could be attributed to Joyce himself. In several cases there was no clear preference between two or more readings and the judgement had to rest on editorial discretion. Few of the more than five thousand alterations to established texts, however, make any great difference to the interpretation of the novel. Most of them are based on punctuation and minor spelling differences, but in some cases phrases and even whole sentences have been restored. Richard Ellmann discusses some of the more interesting corrections in his introduction to the text.

Although the Corrected Text did not claim to be definitive, and indeed elicited some initial criticism from opponents who disagreed with its editorial principles, it was generally more correct than its predecessors. Since Joyce's works passed into the public domain in 2012, there is now a wide range of new reprints and editions to choose from. Today's reader is just as likely to be using a facsimile of the 1922 first edition, a text based on the Odyssey Press edition of 1934 or the Bodley Head edition of 1960, or even the controversial 'Reader's Edition' of 1997 in which the text was not only corrected but also copy-edited to bring Joyce into line with conventional spelling and punctuation.

By general consensus, however, the Corrected Text remains the standard for reference purposes, and the page numbers in the margins of this guide refer to that edition. For those using other editions, the quotations in the Guide may be used as signposts to help locate the corresponding pages in the copy of *Ulysses* in hand.

Appendix III
Joyce's Schema and the Episode Titles

In 1921 Joyce lent Carlo Linati a schema or plan of *Ulysses* in which he assigned to each episode a title from an episode in Homer's *Odyssey*, a time, a colour, persons, a technique, a science or art, a sense or meaning, an organ of the body and a symbol. Joyce also lent it to Valery Larbaud for a lecture, in order, as he said, 'To help him to confuse the audience a little more'. In 1931 Joyce allowed Stuart Gilbert to publish most of the schema in *James Joyce's Ulysses*, with a number of changes (suggesting that parts of the plan were made to fit the book rather than the other way round). The full text of both versions is reproduced in Richard Ellmann's *Ulysses by the Liffey* and can also, of course, be found on the internet.

The information contained in the schema does not convey much in the way of clarification. However, it is referred to occasionally in the Guide where it seems of particular interest. Some of the times given in the plan are misleading, and Joyce himself changed his mind about the times of the later episodes in the second version of the schema. The times quoted in the Guide are taken from the schema only when internal evidence does not suggest otherwise.

The Homeric titles given to the episodes are traditionally used by commentators, although they do not appear in the text of *Ulysses*. Joyce did use them in early drafts and later dropped them, but gave his approval for Stuart Gilbert and Frank Budgen to use the titles in their books. The spelling of some of the Greek names varies according to the commentator.

Appendix IV
Stephen's Morning Itinerary

This guide sticks with the idea that Stephen proceeds from Dalkey to Lansdowne Road station and walks straight down to the beach where the narrative of *Proteus* begins at about 10.40 a.m., and that when the mourners see him in Irishtown half an hour later he is walking towards the city centre. This follows the Linati schema which sets the action of *Proteus* between 10.00 and 11.00 a.m. However a good case has been made by some commentators, including the authors of *James Joyce's Dublin*, for following the later Gilbert schema which sets the episode an hour later, opening a few minutes after *Hades*. With plenty of time in hand after the end of *Nestor*, Stephen could have taken the same train (which at that hour in the real world did not stop at Lansdowne Road) as far as Westland Row. He arrives as the freshly bathed Bloom heads for a tram nearby, follows him on foot along Great Brunswick Street and through Irishtown, and is seen making for the beach as the carriages pass by. As Ian Gunn outlines in his article 'Stephen's stroll on the strand' (*James Joyce Online Notes*, February 2015), he passes Strasburg Terrace, descends to the beach nearby and has already walked some distance past Leahy's Terrace by the time the episode begins. He turns back after opening his eyes, moving closer to the shore as the waves draw nearer, and follows the path described in the guide. The narrative of *Proteus* thus begins at about 11.20. This scenario allows Stephen slightly more time for his walk on the strand, but necessitates the use of a tram to get him back to the city centre and the newspaper office in time for *Aeolus*. It also has him passing Aunt Sara's house no less than three times without going in, having walked all the way back from the city to get there. Joyce may originally have intended the earlier timing and, when later the neat idea of synchronising *Proteus* and *Hades* was introduced, he did not make sufficient alterations to fit the two exactly together.

Bibliography

Harald Beck and John Simpson (editors), *James Joyce Online Notes*, www.jjon.org, 2011 onwards.

Bruce Bidwell and Linda Heffer, *The Joycean Way: A Topographic Guide to Dubliners and a Portrait of the Artist as a Young Man*, Wolfhound Press, 1981.

Harry Blamires, *The Bloomsday Book*, Methuen, 1966.

Jason Bolton, Tim Carey, Rob Goodbody and Gerry Clabby, *The Martello Towers of Dublin,* Dun Laoghaire-Rathdown County Council and Fingal County Council, 2012.

Carole Brown and Leo Knuth, *Bloomsday: The Eleventh Hour – A Quest for the Vacant Place*, A Wake Newslitter Press, 1981.

Frank Budgen, *James Joyce and the Making of Ulysses*, Grayson and Grayson, 1934.

Desmond Clarke, *Dublin*, Batsford, 1977.

Maurice Craig, *Dublin, 1660-1860*, Hodges Figgis, 1952.

Frank Delaney, *James Joyce's Odyssey*, Hodder and Stoughton, 1981.

Richard Ellmann, *James Joyce* (revised edition), Oxford University Press, 1982.

—*Ulysses on the Liffey*, Faber and Faber, 1972.

—*James Joyce's Tower*, Eastern Regional Tourism Organisation, 1969.

Stuart Gilbert, *James Joyce's Ulysses: A Study*, Faber and Faber, 1930.

Oliver St John Gogarty, *It Isn't This Time of Year at All!*, MacGibbon and Kee, 1954.

Clive Hart and Leo Knuth, *A Topographical Guide to James Joyce's Ulysses* (revised and corrected edition), A Wake Newslitter Press, 1981.

Clive Hart and Ian Gunn with Harald Beck, *James Joyce's Dublin: A Topographical Guide to James Joyce's Ulysses*, Thames and Hudson, 2004.

James Joyce, *Ulysses: The Corrected Text*, Penguin Books/The Bodley Head, 1986.

—*Dubliners: The Corrected Text*, Jonathan Cape, 1967.

—*A Portrait of the Artist as a Young Man*, B. W. Huebsch, 1916.

—*Letters of James Joyce, Vol. I* (ed. Stuart Gilbert), Faber and Faber, 1957.

—*Letters of James Joyce, Vol. II and III* (ed. Richard Ellmann), Faber and Faber, 1966.

Weston St John Joyce, *The Neighbourhood of Dublin,* 1912 (revised edition, 1922) Gill.

Terence Killeen, *Ulysses Unbound: A Reader's Companion to James Joyce's Ulysses,* Wordwell, 2004.

Pat Liddy, 'Dublin Today', *Irish Times*.

Frank MacDonald, *The Destruction of Dublin*, Gill and Macmillan, 1985.

National Archives, *Census of Ireland 1901 and 1911,* www.census.nationalarchives.ie, 2008.

Frederick O'Dwyer, *Lost Dublin*, Gill and Macmillan, 1981.

Mary Power, 'The Discovery of *Ruby,*' *James Joyce Quarterly*, Vol. 18, No. 2, 1981.

F. L. Radford, 'King, Pope and Hero-Martyr: Ulysses and the Nightmare of Irish History', *James Joyce Quarterly*, Vol. 15, No. 4, 1978.

Danis Rose, 'The Best Recent Scholarship in Joyce', *James Joyce Quarterly*, Vol. 23, No. 3, 1986.

Weldon Thornton, *Allusions in Ulysses: An Annotated List*, University of North Carolina Press, 1968.

Mervyn Wall, *Forty Foot Gentlemen Only,* Allen Figgis, 1962.

Note: This bibliography is not an exhaustive one. Essentially it is a list of those works consulted or cited specifically in connection with the writing of this book. There are, of course, many other books on Joyce and on Dublin which have contributed to my views and knowledge of the subject over a period of years.

Index

Abbey Street 141, 193
Abbey Street Lower 132, 150,
   216
Abbey Street Middle 12, 51,
   144-47, 149, 151, 162, 216
Amiens Street 84, 92, 217, 218
Abbey Theatre 14, 49, 174-75
Adam Court 158-59
Adrian IV 111
Advertising Company Limited
   50
Aeolus 58, 142-50, 216, 224
Agendath Netaim 63, 66, 165
Aldborough House 75, 76
Alexander & Company, seed
   merchants 139
'All Hallows' (St Andrew's)
   Church 102-3
American Embassy 191
Amiens Street (now Connolly)
   Station 79, 82-84, 174, 193,
   217
Anderson, Micky, watchmaker
   185
Andrew Street 159
Anglesea Road 192-93
Anglesea Street 186-87
Annesley Bridge 77

Antient Concert Rooms 48
Apothecaries' Hall 173
'Araby' 75
Arbour Hill 13, 201
Armstrong 27
Arran Quay 183
Arran Street 137-38, 212, 217
Artane 73
Artifoni, Almidano 105, 124,
   156-57, 176, 191, 216
Aston Quay 125, 153

Bachelor's Walk 13, 125, 146,
   151, 155, 199, 216
Bacon, Sir Francis 170
Bailey Lighthouse 34-35
Bailey Restaurant 160-61
Ball, Sir Robert 153
Ballast office 152, 153, 155
Ballsbridge 34, 105, 151-52, 158
Bank of Ireland, College Green
   (former Parliament House)
   156, 188-89
Bannon, Alec 110-11, 113
Barnacle, Nora 21-22, 104, 106,
   169
Barry, J. M. & Co., tailor 136
Barter, Richard 104

Bassi, J., figure-maker 128
Bath Avenue 191
Bath Street 34, 46, 191
Beach Road 32, 38
Beach, Sylvia 18
Beaufoy, Philip 63
Beaver Street 90, 92, 217, 218
Beck, Harald, and Simpson,
    John 46, 171
Beckett, Samuel 98, 106, 142, 156
Bedford Row 123-26, 157, 186,
    216
Belfast and Oriental Tea
    Company 101
Belvedere College 72
Belvidere Place 74
Bengal Terrace 54
Benson's Ferry 122
Beresford Place 64, 93-94, 97
Bergan, Alf 133, 204-5, 208
Bergin, Dan, publican, Amiens
    Street (now Lloyd's) 92
Bergin, Dan, publican, North
    Strand Road 76
Berkeley Street 52-53
Best, Richard 168
Bidwell, Bruce, and Heffer,
    Linda 213
Blackhall Place 200-1
Blackrock 75, 192
Blanche, Jacques-Emile 114
Blessington Street 52, 62
blind stripling, a 105-6, 132,
    136, 163-64, 178, 190

Bloody Bridge (now Rory
    O'More Bridge) 135, 183,
    199, 200

Bloom, Leopold 7-11, 33-38,
    59-60, 68, 215-18 (Nausikaa)
    13, 29, 31-37, 66, 217
    (Hades) 12, 28, 29, 45-58,
    179, 215, 223-24 (Calypso)
    12, 59-64, 98, 215 (Ithaca)
    13, 59, 64-71, 80, 98-105,
    218 (Circe) 13, 80-92, 166,
    217 (Eumaeus) 13, 80, 92-98,
    218 (Lotuseaters) 12, 80,
    98-105, 215 (Oxen of the
    Sun) 13, 66, 80, 107-14, 217
    (Sirens) 13, 115, 128-41, 184,
    216 (Aeolus) 12, 58, 142-51,
    216, 224 (Laestrygonians) 12,
    142, 151-66, 216 (Scylla and
    Charybdis) 12, 142, 166-76,
    216 (Cyclops) 13, 138, 193,
    201-12, 216
Bloom, Marcus, dentist 106
Bloom, Milly 63, 65, 111,
    112
Bloom, Molly 19, 35, 49, 63,
    67-71, 89, 97, 103, 121, 123,
    133, 137, 160, 162, 176
Bloom, Rudolph 56
Bloom, Rudy 55, 68, 91, 105
'Boarding House, The' 205
Boardman, Edy and baby
    32-33
Bodega Co. Wine Stores 127,
    186
Boland's Mill 48
Bolton, W., grocer 155
Bolton Street 212
Bonham Street 199
Botanic Gardens 55
Boulger, James 102

Bow Bridge 195
Bow Lane 196
Boyd, druggist 131
Boylan, Hugh 'Blazes' 12, 48-50, 63, 65, 68-71, 87, 89, 96, 116, 118, 121, 129, 131-33, 135, 153, 161-62, 164, 176-78, 190, 208
Brady, Joe 147
Brady's Cottages 100
Brandes, George 170
Bray Head 20
Brayden, William 145
Breen, Denis 155, 188, 199, 205, 208, 209
Breen, Josie 83, 154-55, 188, 199, 205
Breffni Road 25
Bremen Grove 39, 41
Brian Boroimh, pub 54
Broadbent, J. S., fruiterer 190
Brown, Carole, and Knuth, Leo 47, 123, 213
Brown, Thomas & Co., silk merchants, 159, 178
Brunswick Street, North 202-3
Brunswick Street, Great (now Pearse Street) 48, 100, 101, 223
Budgen, Frank 32, 69, 114, 160, 222, 225
Bullock, Harbour and Castle 19, 25
Bully's Acre 195
Burgh Quay 50, 118, 126
Burgh, Thomas 196
Burke, Edmund 156

Burke, J., publican 87, 112-13, 190, 217
Burke, Thomas 148
Burton Restaurant 161
Bushe, Seymour 148
Butler, James, Duke of Ormonde 193
Butt Bridge 98-99, 218
Byrne, Davy, publican 161-63, 216
Byrne, J. F. ('Cranly') 59, 67, 121, 153, 173

cabman's shelter, nr. Butt Bridge 94-97
cabman's shelter, nr. Westland Row Station 101
Caffrey, Cissy 32-34, 82, 89-90
Caffrey, Tommy and Jacky 32-34
Cahill's corner 141, 184
Callan, Nurse 108, 111
Calypso 12, 59-64, 98, 215
Camden Hall 175
Cantrell and Cochrane 101
Cantwell's, wine merchants 128
Capel Street 128-29, 140, 202, 205, 212
Carey, James 147
Carr, Henry 90
Carr, Private 82, 89-91
Carroll, J., jeweller 128
Castleyard Gate, Upper 115-16
Cats' and Dogs' Home 48
Cattle Market 202
Cavendish, Lord Frederick 147
Cecilia Street 121

Central Bank 186
Ceppi, P., statuary maker 129
Chambers, Sir William 79
Chancery Street (Pill Lane) 138, 202, 216
Chandler, Thomas 'Little' 159, 212
Chapelizod 181
Chapterhouse, St Mary's Abbey 138-40
Charlemont, Lord 79
Charles Street 137, 183-84
Charleville Mall 77
Chesterfield, Lord 179
Chicken Lane 201
Childs murder, the 54
Christ Church Cathedral 184
Church Avenue 191
Church Street 202-3
Circe 13, 80-92, 166, 217
Citizen, the 6-11, 31, 58, 69, 205
City Arms Hotel 201-2
City Hall 115-16, 141, 184, 209
City Quay 98
Civic Offices 129
Clare Street 106, 190
Clarence Hotel 129
Clements, Nathaniel 179
Clery's, drapers 101
Clifford, Martha 67, 101, 129, 134, 135
Clifton School 26
Clohissey, M., bookseller 123, 124, 169
Clongowes Wood College 39, 73, 78, 112
Clontarf, Battle of 54
Cochrane 26-27, 101
Cock Lake 43

Cohen, Bella 10, 85-88, 90, 168, 217
Coleraine Street 203
College Green 44, 125, 146, 156-58, 171, 175, 187-88, 215, 216
College Park 105, 190
College Street 155, 189
Collis and Ward, solicitors 188
Colum, Padraic 17
Combridge's, stationers 160
Commercial Buildings 186-87
Compton, Private 82, 89-91
Conmee, very Rev. John 12, 58, 73-79, 112, 125
Connellan, Rev. Thomas, bookseller 163
Connolly, James 94
Conroy, Gabriel and Gretta 52
Conway's (now Kennedy's) pub 101, 103
Cooley, Thomas 184
Cork Hill 115-16, 212
Corless's Restaurant 159
Corley, 'Lord' John 94
Cormack, T., publican 83
Costello, Frank 'Punch' 109, 111
'Counterparts' 119
Cowley, Father Bob 135, 140, 199
Crampton Court 13, 117-18, 132, 163, 185
Crampton, Sir Philip 49, 117, 189
Crane Street 199
Cranly *see* Byrne, J. F.
Crawford, Myles 140, 145-49, 209

Creation Arcade 163-64
Crimmins, W. C., publican 196-97
Crofton 211
Cromwell's Quarters 195
Crosbie and Alleyne's 119
Crossguns Bridge 53
Crosthwaite Park 171
Crotthers, J. 111
Crown Alley 186
Cuchulain, statue 142
Cumberland Street, South 48
Cunningham, Martin 13, 45, 47, 52, 57-58, 115-16, 135, 205, 207, 210-11
Cunningham Road 28
Curran, Sarah 207
Cusack, Michael 73, 204
Cussen, Cliodna 37, 49
Custom House 93-95, 97
Cyclops 13, 138, 193, 210-16, 216

Dalkey 24-27, 29, 157, 215, 223
Dalkey Avenue 12, 25-26, 28, 215
Dalkey Heritage Centre 25
Dalkey Station 28
Daly, Teresa, tobacconist 129-30
Daly's Club 187
Dalymount Park 53
Dame Gate 185
Dame Lane 187
Dame Street 13, 118, 120, 127, 153, 158, 185-86, 188-89, 199
Dana magazine 167, 174
Davis, Thomas, statue 189
Dawson, Dan 145
Dawson Street 106, 163, 189-90

DBC (Dublin Bakery Company) Restaurant 13, 121, 140, 158, 175, 185
'Dead, The' 52, 189, 200
Deane, Sir Thomas 164
Deasy, Garret 26-28, 43, 89, 97, 109, 146, 169, 215
Dedalus, Boody 12, 53, 69
Dedalus, Dilly 13, 152, 185
Dedalus, Katey 12, 53, 69
Dedalus, Maggy 53
Dedalus, Simon 13, 47, 54, 95, 126-27, 131-34, 139, 145-46, 184, 199
Dedalus, Stephen 13, 47, 54, 95, 126-27, 131-34, 139, 145-46, 184, 199 (*Telemachus*) 12, 14-25, 215 (*Nestor*) 12, 26-28, 215, 223 (*Proteus*) 29, 37-44, 215, 223, 224 (*Ithaca*) 13, 59, 64-71, 80, 98, 218 (*Circe*) 13, 80-91, 166, 217 (*Eumaeus*) 13, 80, 92-98, 218 (*Oxen of the Sun*) 13, 66, 80, 107-14, 217 (*Aeolus*) 12, 58, 142-50, 216 (*Scylla and Charybdis*) 12, 142, 166-76, 216
De Massey, Nora 130
Denzille Lane 217, 112, 113
Denzille (now Fenian) Street 113
Dervorgilla 209
De Selby 25
De Valera, Eamon 48
Dignam, Master Patrick 13, 36, 123, 177-78, 190
Dignam, Mrs 208
Dignam, Paddy 29, 31, 78, 115, 205, 213

Dignam residence 36, 47, 135

Dillon, John, MP 72

Dillon's auctionrooms 124-26, 146, 148-49

Dineen, Father Patrick 173

Distillery Stores 199

Dixon 109, 111, 113

Dlugacz, Moses 62, 70, 215

Dock Tavern (now The Bow Dock) 93

Dodd, Reuben, J. 51, 127, 137, 183

Dodder River 29, 47

D'Olier Street 12, 50, 51, 132, 189, 217

Dollard, Ben 87, 127, 133-34, 136, 186

Dollard House 184

Dolphin Hotel 118

Donnelly, Ignatius 170

Donnycarney 125

Donohoe's pub 177, 178, 212

Doran, Bob 116, 158, 177-78, 204-5, 208

Doran, M., publican 164

Dorset Street 52, 59, 62, 71, 72, 133, 177, 212

Douce, Lydia 116, 130-31, 133-36, 184

Doyle, J. C. 48

Doyle, Madame, milliner 178

Drago, A., hairdresser 164

Dublin Castle 13, 115, 129, 212

Dublin Civic Museum 50, 189, 206

Dublin Woollen Company 126

Dublin Writers Museum 52

Dubliners 48, 57, 73, 75, 94, 119, 134, 147, 159, 167, 178, 200, 205, 211, 212, 213

Dudley, Lord Robert 170

Duke Lane 161, 163

Duke Street 160, 163

Dun Laoghaire (formerly Kingstown) 14, 19, 34, 36, 41, 171, 192

Dunne, Miss 12, 50, 177

Dunphy's (now Doyle's) Corner 53, 58

Earl Street, North 150

East Link Toll Bridge 122

Eccles Street 10, 12, 13, 53, 59, 61-64, 71-72, 101, 123, 133, 136, 160, 177, 212, 215, 218

Eccles Lane 66

Eden Quay 96, 99, 132, 151, 216

Edward VII 91, 207

Egan, Kevin 41

Egan, Patrice 40

Eglinton, John (W. K. Magee) 167, 169, 171-72

elderly female, no longer young 123

Elizabeth I 156, 170

Ellmann, Richard 220, 221

Elvery's Elephant House 51

Ely Place 110, 112

Emmet, Robert 137, 198, 204, 207

Empire Buffet (now Lillie's Bordello) 158, 177

Empire Musichall (now Olympia Theatre) 117, 118

Esposito, Miss 175

Essex Gate 13, 115, 185
Essex Street 185, 116, 119
Eumaeus 13, 80, 92-98, 218
Eustace Street 119
Evening Telegraph, The 12, 28, 36, 55, 70, 96, 145-49, 151
Exchequer Street 178

Fairview 127, 77
Falkiner, Sir Frederick 164
Fanning, long John 116, 127, 188
Farrell, Cashel Boyle O'Connor Fitzmaurice Tisdall 13, 105, 155, 174, 190
Farrington 119
Fay brothers 175
Fenians 195
Ferguson, Sir Samuel 72
Figatner, Aaron, jeweller 128
Findlater's Church 52
Finglas Road 54
Finnegans Wake 166, 181
Finn's Hotel 104, 106, 176
Fitzgerald, Desmond 140
Fitzgerald, Francis, bookseller 123
Fitzgerald, 'Silken Thomas' 140
Fitzgibbon, Lord Justice Gerald 110
Fitzgibbon Street 75
Fitzharris, 'Skin-the-Goat' 58, 95, 147
Five Lamps 75
Fleet Street 13, 123, 124, 155, 216
Fleischmann, Marthe 135

Flower, Henry 86, 87, 101
Flynn, Nosey 111, 161, 162, 163, 185
Forty Foot bathing place 17, 20, 22, 24, 215
Four Courts 122, 123, 129, 137-38, 183
Fownes Street 120-22, 185-86
Frederick Street, North 133, 52
Frederick Street, South 105
Free Church 75
Freeman's Journal, The 10, 12, 100-1, 135, 143-45, 149, 204
Freemason's Hall 164

Gallagher, W., grocer 75
Gallaher, Ignatius 147
Gandon, James 93, 137, 156
Gardiner Place 64, 73, 218
Gardiner Street 12, 53, 64, 71, 74, 218
Gardner, Lieutenant Stanley 70
Gasworks 48
Gate Theatre 52
Gaudens, Augustus Saint 52
General Post Office 51, 142-43
General Slocum 198
George IV 19
George's Quay 98
Geraghty, Michael 201
Gibbons, Grinling 189
Gill, M. H. & Son, booksellers 121, 168
Gillen, P., hairdresser 83
Glasnevin (Prospect) Cemetery 53-57
Globe Theatre 168

Gogarty, Oliver St John 16, 17, 19, 21, 52, 72, 124, 160, 225

Goodwin, Professor 89

Goulding, Richie 38, 122, 129, 132-35, 183

'Grace' 73

Grafton Street 116, 153, 158-89, 161, 167, 176-78, 189

Grand Canal 47, 190

Grattan (Essex) Bridge 127, 129, 130, 140, 177, 184

Gray, John, Sir, statue 51, 144, 149

Great Charles Street 75

Great George's Street, North 62, 72

Great Strand Street 141

Greek Street 136, 138, 216

Green Street and Courthouse 135, 188, 203-5, 216

Greene, Roger, solicitor 129

Gresham Hotel 52

Griffith, Arthur 17, 160, 211

Griffith Avenue 79

Grosvenor Hotel 101

Guinness, Arthur 198

Guinness Brewery 150, 152, 183, 197, 198

Haddington Road 178, 190-91, 215

Hades 12, 28, 45-59, 179, 223-24

Haines 13-14, 19-24, 91, 95, 111, 121, 150, 168-71, 174-75

Halfpenny (Metal) Bridge 122, 126, 127, 186

Halston Street 203

Hanover Street 100

Hardwicke Place 62, 64, 72

Harris, Frank 170

Harrison, C. W. 176

Harrison's Restaurant 154

Hart, Clive, and Knuth, Leo 123, 128, 169, 184, 191

Hathaway, Ann 169, 170, 172

Hawkins Street 118

Hely's men 153, 176, 189

Henrietta Street 212

Henry II 111

Henry VIII 111

Henry, Jimmy 115

Henry and James, clothiers 185

Henry Street 150, 212

Herzog, Moses 202

Heseltine, Lieutenant colonel H. G. 179

Higgins, Zoe 86-89

Holles Street 37, 83, 105-7, 113-14, 134,

Holles Street Hospital (National Maternity Hospital) 13, 87, 108, 132, 146, 155, 190, 216, 217

Hornblower 104, 190

Horne, Dr Andrew 107

Howth Head 19, 34, 36, 71, 162

Howth Road 77

Hughes, Harry 65

Humble, William, Earl of Dudley see viceroy 179

Huston, John 200

Hyde, Douglas 42, 121

Hynes, Joe 55, 56, 96, 145, 201-5, 207, 209-11

Irish Catholic and Penny Journal, The 149
Irish Homestead, The 167, 169
Irish Independent, The 149, 204
Irish Literary Theatre 174
Irish Times, The 155
Irishtown 38, 44, 47, 146, 155, 215, 223
Irishtown Road 44, 46, 47
Irish Volunteers 142
Irwin, Francis 26
Island Street 199
Ithaca 13, 59, 64-71, 80, 98, 218
Ivory, Thomas 200
Ivy Church 77
'Ivy Day in the Committee Room' 178, 211

James's Gate 197
James's Street 13, 126, 195-97
Jammet's 158-59
Johnston, Francis 62, 142, 187, 195
Joyce, James 7-11, 17, 19-22, 25-27, 29, 32, 33, 35-37, 44, 48, 52, 55, 56-59, 62, 72-75, 77, 83, 90, 93, 100, 102, 104, 107, 114, 121, 124, 126, 130, 131, 133-35, 140, 144, 147-50, 156-57, 160, 162-63, 165-67, 168, 169, 172, 175, 187, 190, 192, 193, 201, 207, 212, 219, 220, 221, 222, 223, 224
Joyce, James, Cultural Centre 4, 62, 72, 161

Joyce, James, Institute of Ireland 56
Joyce, James, Museum 16, 18
Joyce, Weston St John 17, 39, 42, 44, 77
Jury's Hotel 187

Kane, Matthew 58
Kavanagh, James, publican (now The Turk's Head) 116, 127, 184
Kavanagh, Patrick 160
Kelleher, Corny 12, 76, 90-91, 208-9
Kendall, Marie 185
Kennedy, J. & C., rectifiers 128
Kennedy, Mina 116, 130, 131, 134, 136, 184
Kennedy, Peter, hairdresser 198
Keogh-Bennett match 178
Kerlogue Road 39
Kernan, Tom 13, 54-55, 126, 134, 183, 196-200
Kettle, Thomas 74
Keyes, Alexander 126, 129, 145-46, 148-49, 152, 163, 171, 208, 216
Kiernan, Barney, publican 13, 23, 31, 96, 132, 137-38, 141, 202-4, 206, 216, 217
Kildare Street 12, 164, 166, 175-76, 216
Kildare Street Club 105, 128, 176, 188
Kilkenny People, The 171
Killiney 20
Kilmainham Gaol 95

Kilmainham Lane 195
King Street, North 203
Kingsbridge 182, 193
Kingsbridge (now Heuston) Station 182
King's Hospital 'Bluecoat' School 200
King's Inns 212, 148
Kirk, Thomas 150
Kish lightship 36

Laestrygonians 12, 142, 151-67, 216
Lambay Island 111
Lambert, Ned 13, 54-55, 126, 139-41, 145-46, 149, 198, 208, 211
Land League 195
Lansdowne Road 28, 29, 191, 215
Larchet's Hotel 87, 125, 187, 216
Leahy's Terrace 28, 30-32, 34, 37-38
Leask, H.M. & Co., linseed crushers 98-99
Lee, Sidney 170
Le Fanu, Sheridan 114
Leinster House 106, 114, 165, 192
Leinster Street 12, 13, 104, 215
Leitrim, Lord 202
Lemon, Graham, confectioner 151
Lenehan, T. 13, 51, 94, 109, 112-13, 118, 120, 122, 128-29, 131-33, 146-47, 162-63, 177, 184, 209-10

Leonard, Hugh 25
Leonard, Paddy 163
Leo X 207
Léon, Paul 72, 166
Levenston's dancing academy 105
Lewis, Wyndham 114
Liberties, The 205
Liberty Hall 94
Lidwell, George 134-36
Liffey River 39, 43, 51, 129, 150, 193
Liffey Street, Lower 126, 141
Lime Street 99-100
Lincoln Place 101, 103-4, 113, 190, 215
Lincoln Place Baths 104
Linenhall Barracks 202-3
Lisburn Street 203
Little Britain Street 13, 138, 141, 204, 212, 216
'Little Cloud, A' 147, 159, 212
Little Green Street 138, 141, 212, 216, 217
Lombard Street, East 48, 100
Londonbridge Road 191
Long, John, publican 164
Longworth, Ernest 175
Loop Line Bridge 82, 84, 93
Loré, Prosper, hat manufacturer 128
Lotts, North 141
Lotuseaters 12, 80, 98-105, 215
Love, Reverend Hugh C. 127-28, 139, 140, 184
Lundy Foot, tobacconists 184-85
Lurgan Street 203

Lynam, bookmaker 120
Lyons, Frederick 'Bantam' 103-4, 113, 120, 163
Lyster, T. W. 166-73

Mabbot Street (now James Joyce Street) 80, 83, 217
McCabe, Archbishop 54
McCarthy, Denis Florence 26
MacConnell, A., chemist 71
McCormack, John 48
M'Coy, C. P. 13, 97, 101, 120, 122, 128-29, 132, 163, 184
MacDowell, Gerty 32-36, 83, 129, 184
MacHugh, Professor 145-48
M'Intosh (man in the macintosh) 55, 97, 113, 190
McKenna, Jakki 126
Mack, Mrs Annie 80, 86
MacMurrough, Dermot 209
Madden, O. 146
Magazine Fort 181
Maginni, Denis J. 72, 89, 123, 189
Maison Claire, La 158, 177-78
Malahide Road 77-79
Mangan, P., porkbutcher 123, 177-78
Marino Casino 78-79
Marino Crescent 77
Marino Estate 78
Marks, Lionel, antique dealer 130, 137-38, 216
Martello Tower, Sandycove (Joyce Tower) 12, 14-23, 26, 32, 41, 43, 63, 95, 125, 167, 171, 215

Mary Street 131, 173, 212
Mary's Abbey 13, 128, 138-39, 140-41
Mary's Lane 138, 216
Mater Misericordiae Hospital 53, 59, 61, 62, 109
Meade's timberyard 48
Meetinghouse Lane 138
Menton, John Henry 55, 57, 154, 186, 187-88
Merchants' Arch 13, 120, 122, 123, 128, 177, 186, 216
Merrion Hall 13, 106, 113, 151
Merrion Square 13, 105-7, 110, 114, 178, 190
Metropole Hotel 143
Military Road 193, 195
milkwoman, the 22
Miller, William, plumber 163
Mirus Bazaar 34, 36, 164
Moira Hotel 125, 186, 187
Molesworth Street 164
Montgomery (now Foley) Street 80, 84, 92
Mooney's *en ville* 87, 132, 216
Mooney's *sur mer* 87, 99, 132, 151
Moore, George 110, 112, 169, 174-75
Moore, Thomas, statue 154, 156
Morkan, Julia and Kate 200
Moses, Marcus Tertius, tea merchant 119
Moulang, D., jeweller and pipe importer 128
Mount Brown 195
Mount Street, Lower 190
Mountjoy Square 64, 73-75

Mud Island 77
Muglins, the 19-20
Mullett, J., publican 92
Mulligan, Malachi 'Buck' 13,
    14-24, 44, 89, 91, 95, 109-13,
    121, 124, 128, 150, 165, 169-75
Mulvey, Harry 70
Murphy, D. B., redbearded
    sailor 95-96
Murray, Josephine 36
Murray, Red 145

Nameless One, The 138, 201-11
Nannetti, Councillor J. P. 58,
    129, 145, 163, 208-9
Nassau Street 105-6, 128, 158,
    175-78, 189-90
National Gallery of Ireland
    106, 114
National Library of Ireland 16,
    31, 46, 57, 61, 74, 76, 78, 84,
    94, 99, 102, 116, 119, 130,
    144, 152, 154, 157, 159, 182,
    183, 188
National Museum of Ireland
    128, 162,164-65, 170-71, 175,
    183, 193, 216
Nausikaa 13, 29, 31-37, 66,
    217
Nelson Street 72, 122
Nelson's Pillar 142, 144, 149
Nestor 12, 14, 26-28, 215, 223
Newbridge Avenue 28, 29, 31,
    44, 46, 212, 215, 217
Newcomen Bridge 77
Newgate Gaol 76, 204
Nichols, J. & C., undertakers 100
Nighttown 67, 77, 80, 82, 83, 124

Nolan, John Wyse 115-16,
    184-85, 209-11
North Circular Road 53, 58, 75,
    201-2
North City Market 202
North Star Hotel 92
North Strand Road 12, 75, 79
Northumberland Road 191
North Wall 199
Nymph, the 88
O'Beirne Bros., publicans 83
Oblong, May 80

O'Brien, Flann 25
O'Brien Institute 78-79
O'Brien, William Smith, statue 51
O'Casey, Seán 62, 98, 212
O'Connell Bridge 50-51, 125,
    151-52, 177, 189, 199, 212,
    217
O'Connell, Daniel 51, 114
O'Connell, John 55
O'Connell (Sackville) Street
    51, 121, 123, 133, 141-44,
    149-51, 153, 168, 212, 216
O'Doherty, Eamonn 94
O'Donohoe, M. 'Ruggy',
    publican, The International
    Bar 177-78
O'Dwyer, Frederick 189
Odyssey 82, 95, 103, 109, 144,
    161, 168, 206, 220, 221
O'Hare, Doctor 108-9
Old Gummy Granny 91
Old Quarry 25-26
Olhausen, W., porkbutcher 5,
    10, 11
O'Madden Burke, Mr 146

O'Molloy, J. J. 71, 139-41, 145, 148-49

O'Neill, H. J., undertaker 76

O'Neill, J. J., publican (now The Norseman) 119

onelegged sailor, the 12, 69, 71, 122

Ormond Hotel 13, 38, 105, 116, 118, 123, 126-30, 134, 137, 177, 200, 209, 212, 216

Ormond Quay, Lower 127

Ormond Quay, Upper 127, 129-30, 136-38, 183

O'Rourke, Larry, publican (now the Aurora) 62

O'Shea brothers 176

O'Shea, Kitty 97

O'Sullivan, Sean 114

O'Sullivan, Seamus 17

Ouzel Galley 186-87

Oval, The, pub 126, 139, 146

Oxen of the Sun 13, 66, 80, 107-14, 217

'Painful Case, A' 52, 57

Palmerstown 200

Palmieri, Benedetto 157, 191

'Parable of the Plums, The' 65, 148

Parkgate 181-82

Parliament Street 115-16, 185, 212

Parnell, Charles Stewart 52, 56, 97, 121, 160, 195; grave 56; monument 52

Parnell, John Howard 121, 140, 158

Pat the waiter 132-36

Pearce, Sir Edward Lovett 156

Pearse, Patrick 49, 142

Penelope 13, 59, 68-71, 171, 218

Phibsborough Road 53

Philip Drunk and Philip Sober 87

Phoenix Monument 179

Phoenix Park 13, 58, 147, 153, 179, 180, 182

Pigeonhouse, the 39, 40, 42

Pigeonhouse Road 32, 37, 40, 44

Pigott & Co., musical instrument sellers 189

Pine Road 41

Pitt, William, the Younger 14

Pius X 207

Plumtree's Potted Meat 23, 161

Police Gazette, The 209

Ponsonby, E., bookseller 189

Poolbeg lighthouse 34

Poolbeg Road 41, 44

Poddle River 184

Portland Row 75

Portrait of the Artist as a Young Man, A, 54, 59, 72-74, 156, 166, 178

Post offices: College Green 44, 146, 215; Molesworth Street 164; Ormond Quay 136; Sir John Rogerson's Quay 98; Westland Row 103

Power, Jack 47, 54, 56, 115, 116, 211

Powerhouse, Fleet Street 124

Prince's Stores 144
Prince's Street 12, 143-44
Proteus 12, 29, 37-44, 215, 223, 224
Provost's house 158, 177, 190
Prussia Street 201-2
Pulbrook Robertson, tea importers 198
Purdon Street 84
Purefoy, Mina 35, 37, 108-9, 111, 155

Queen's Bridge 183
Queen's Hotel, Ennis 65
Queen's Theatre 49
Queen Victoria 191
Quigley, Nurse 110

Rabaiotti, Antonio, restaurateur 71, 83
Radford, F. L. 207
Read, Thomas & Co., cutlers 185
Reade, Amye 163
Red Bank Restaurant 50
Reddy, R. and Daughter, antique dealers 127
Richie, Ian 150
Richmond Bridge 183
Richmond Hospital 202-3
Richmond Street, North 75
Ricketts, Kitty 86-88, 91, 97
Ringsend 39, 47, 215
Ringsend Park 37, 39-40, 44, 46
Ringsend Road 47
Roberts, George 134
Rochford, Tom 117-18, 132-33, 163, 185, 188

Rose, Danis 37
Rotunda Concert Rooms (now the Ambassador) 52
Rover cycleshop 153
Rowe, A., wine and spirit merchant 155
Royal Barracks 182, 193
Royal Canal 47, 39, 215
Royal Dublin Society 191
Royal Hospital, Kilmainham 193, 195
Ruby: The Pride of the Ring 63
Rumbold, Horace 207
Russell, T., lapidary 124
Russell, George 'A.E.' 17, 112, 114, 158, 167-69, 172
Rutland (now Parnell) Square 21, 52
Ryan (or O'Ryan), Terry (barman) 205, 209-10

Sackville Street *see* O'Connell Street
St Andrew's Church, 'All Hallows' 102
St Andrew's School 48
St Catherine's Church 198
St Francis Xavier's Church 73-74
St George's Church 62, 72
St John Chrysostomos 19
St Joseph's Church 75
St Mark's Church 49
St Mary's Church 212
St Michan's Church 202
St Patrick's Hospital 196
St Paul's Church 198
St Peter's Road and Terrace 12, 53, 125

Salkeld, Cecil 161
Salmon, Dean 158
Salvation Army Hall 100
Sandycove 12, 32, 114, 192
Sandycove Avenue 14
Sandycove Bathers' Association 24
Sandycove Point 14, 16, 19-20
Sandycove Station 14, 174
Sandymount 31, 36, 66, 105, 108, 114, 135, 190, 212, 215
Sandymount Avenue 192
Sandymount Road 28, 30
Sandymount Strand 12, 13, 82, 125
Sandymount Tower 32, 41
Sargent, Cyril 27
Sceptre 120, 132, 146, 162, 209
Scotch House 126
Scott, Michael 14, 93
Scylla and Charybdis 12, 142, 166-76, 216
Semple, George 196
Serpentine Avenue 192
Sewell, Son and Simpson, veterinary surgeons 105
Sexton, Walter, goldsmith 158
Shackleton, G. and Sons, flour millers197
Shakespeare, William 89, 167-74
Sheares brothers 201-2, 204
Sheehy family 74-75
Shelbourne Road 29, 192
Sheppard, Oliver 142
Sheridan, Richard Brinsley 212
Ship, The, pub 24, 154, 171, 174
Signal House, The, pub (now Cleary's) 92

Simmonscourt Road 192
Sinico, Emily 52, 57
Sinn Féin 211
Sir John Rogerson's Quay 12, 98-99, 199, 215
Sirens 13, 115, 128-41, 184, 216
Skeffington, Francis Sheehy 74
Slattery, W., publican (Suffolk House) 211
Smirke, Sir William 181
Smith, Law, barrister 105-6
Smithfield 193, 203
Solomons, M.E., optician 106, 190
Speck, Paul 22
Sport 146, 162
Star of the Sea Church 31-36
Steevens, Grissel and Dr Richard; hospital, 196
Steevens' Lane 196
Stephen Hero 153
Stephen's Green 176, 189
Stephenson, Sam 186
Stoker, Bram 77
Stoneybatter 201, 203
Stoppard, Tom 90
Store Street 14, 93, 218
Strand Road 32
Strand Street 39, 44
Strasburg Terrace 38, 40, 44, 223
Subsheriff's office 127, 129, 131, 133, 188, 205
Sunlight Chambers 184
Sweets of Sin 123, 128
Sweny, F. W., chemist 102-3

Swift, Jonathan 156, 196
Swift's Row 126-27
Sycamore Street 118
Sydney Parade Station 57
Synge, John Millington 171

Talbot 27
Talbot, Florry 86-89
Talbot Street 13, 82-84, 217
Tangier Lane 176
Tara Street Station 174, 193
Taxil, Léo 40
Taylor, John F. 148
Telemachus 12, 14-25, 215
Temple Bar 116, 120, 122-23,
    132, 163, 176, 186
Temple Street 64, 72-73, 218
Theosophical Society 169
Thomas Street 198
Thornton, J., fruiterer 12, 50,
    69, 176
Throwaway 23, 65, 104, 120,
    209-10
Titbits 63
Tolka River 77
Tone, Wolfe 201, 212; statue
    176
Townsend Street 100
Trench, Samuel Chenevix 19,
    21-22
Trinity College, Dublin 12, 72,
    101-2, 104, 121, 156, 177,
    189-90, 216
Trinity Street 125, 186-87, 216
Tritonville Road 30, 46, 192
Troy of the D. M. P. 201
Turkish and Warm Baths 104
'Two Gallants' 52, 94

Tyrone Street (now Railway
    Street) 85, 92, 217

Ulverton Road 25
United Irishman, The 210
United Irishmen 198
Usher's Island 200
Viceregal Lodge 122, 179-80
viceroy, viceregal cavalcade 106,
    116, 122, 126, 129, 134, 141,
    158, 178-92
Vico Road 26-27
Virag, Lipoti 86-87
Volta Cinema 131, 212

Walsh, Archbishop William 54
Wandering Rocks i 73-79; ii 76; iii
    71-73; iv 53; v 176-78; vi 156-
    58; vii 50; viii 72, 137-41; ix
    117-23; x 122-23; xi 125-26; xii
    197-99; xiii 124-25; xiv 127-28,
    186; xv 115-22; xvi 120-22; xvii
    105-7; xviii 177-78; xix 179-92
Wapping Street, New 122
Watery Lane (now Dermot
    O'Hurley Avenue) 44, 47
Watling Street 13, 195, 197-99
Wellesley, Arthur 62
Wellington Quay 13, 128, 184,
    186, 216
Wellington Testimonial 181-82
Werner, Lewis, oculist 107
Westland Row 82-3, 93, 95,
    100-3, 112-13, 217, 223
Westmoreland Street 50-51,
    152-54, 189
White, Dudley 183
Whitworth Bridge 183

Wicklow Hotel 178
Wicklow Street 13, 123, 159,
    177-78
Wilde, Oscar 49, 72, 106, 156, 170
Wilde, Sir William 106
Williams's Row (now Bachelors
    Way) 125-26, 146, 149
William Street, South 178
William III, statue 157-58,
    188-89
Windmill Lane 98-99

Windsor Avenue 77, 127
Wine, B., antique dealer 128
Wood Quay 129, 184
Woodward and Deane 176

Yeates and Son, opticians 158
Yeats, William Butler 17, 114,
    167, 192
Youkstetter, W., porkbutcher 76

Zoological Gardens 179